THE COMING CENTURY OF PEACE

THE COMING CENTURY OF PEACE

MIKHAIL S. GORBACHEV

RICHARDSON & STEIRMAN

1986

TABLE OF CONTENTS

Part II. Domestic Policy

THE COMING
CENTURY OF PEACE

PART I
FOREIGN POLICY

1

ADDRESS
TO THE PEOPLE
OF THE UNITED STATES

Esteemed citizens of the
United States of America,
I see a good augury in the way we are beginning the New
Year, which has been declared the year of peace. We are start-
ing it with an exchange of direct messages—President Reagan's
to the Soviet people and mine to you.

This, I believe, is a hopeful sign of change which, though
small, is nonetheless a change for the better in our relations. The
few minutes that I will be speaking to you strike me as a meaningful symbol of our mutual willingness to go on moving toward
each other, which is what your President and I began doing at
Geneva. For a discussion along those lines we had the mandate
of our peoples. They want the constructive Soviet-American
dialogue to continue uninterrupted and to yield tangible results.

As I face you today, I want to say that Soviet people are
dedicated to peace—that supreme value equal to the gift of life.
We cherish the idea of peace, having suffered for it. Together
with the pain of unhealing wounds and the agony of irretrievable
losses, it has become part and parcel of our flesh and blood. In
our country there is not a single family or a single home that has
not kept alive the memory of their kith and kin who perished in
the flames of war—the war in which the Soviet and American
peoples were allies and fought side by side.

I say this because our common quest for peace has its roots
in the past, and that means we have an historic record of cooperation which can today inspire our joint efforts for the sake of the
future.

The many letters I have received from you and my conversations with your fellow countrymen—senators, congress-
men, scientists, businessmen and statesmen—have convinced
me that in the United States, too, people realize that our two
nations should never be at war, that a collision between them
would be the greatest of tragedies.

It is a reality of today's world that it is senseless to seek greater security for oneself through new types of weapons. At present, every new step in the arms race increases the danger and the risk for both sides, and for all humankind.

It is the forceful and compelling demand of life itself that we should follow the path of cutting back nuclear arsenals and keeping outer space peaceful. This is what we are negotiating about at Geneva, and we would very much like those talks to be successful this year.

In our efforts for peace we should be guided by an awareness of the fact that today history has willed our two nations to bear an enormous responsibility to the peoples of our two countries and, indeed, the peoples of all countries, for preserving life on Earth. Our duty to all humankind is to offer it a safe prospect of peace, a prospect of entering the Third Millennium without fear. Let us commit ourselves to doing away with the threat hanging over humanity. Let us not shift that task onto our children's shoulders.

We can hardly succeed in attaining that goal unless we begin saving up, bit by bit, the most precious capital there is— trust among nations and peoples. And it is absolutely essential to start mending the existing deficit of trust in Soviet-American relations.

I believe that one of the main results of my meeting with President Reagan is that, as leaders and as human beings, we were able to take the first steps toward overcoming mistrust and to activate the factor of confidence. The gap dividing us is still wide, to bridge it will not be easy, but we saw in Geneva that it can be done. Bridging that gap would be a great feat—a feat our people are ready to perform for the sake of world peace.

I am reminded of the title of a remarkable work of American literature, the novel *The Winter of Our Discontent*. In that phrase let me just substitute "hope" for "discontent." And may not only this winter but every season of this year and of the years to come be full of hope for a better future, a hope that, together, we can turn into reality. I can assure you that we shall spare no effort in working for that.

For the Soviet people, the year 1986 marks the beginning of

a new stage in carrying out our constructive plans. Those are peaceful plans; we have made them known to the whole world.

I wish you a happy New Year. To every American family I wish good health, peace and happiness.

January 1, 1986

2

NUCLEAR DISARMAMENT
BY THE YEAR 2000

THE NEW YEAR 1986 has started to elapse. It will be an important year, one can say a turning point in the history of the Soviet state, the year of the Twenty-seventh Congress of the CPSU. The Congress will chart the guidelines for the political, social, economic and spiritual development of Soviet society in the period up to the next millennium. It will adopt a program for accelerating our peaceful construction.

All efforts of the CPSU are directed toward ensuring a further improvement in the life of the Soviet people.

A turn for the better is also needed in the international arena. This is the expectation and the demand of the peoples of the Soviet Union and of peoples throughout the world.

Being aware of this, at the start of the new year the Politburo of the CPSU Central Committee and the Soviet Government have adopted a decision on a number of major foreign policy actions of a fundamental nature. They are designed to promote to a maximum degree an improvement in the international situation. They are prompted by the need to overcome the negative, confrontational trends that have been growing in recent years and to clear the ways toward curbing the nuclear arms race on Earth and preventing it in outer space, toward an overall reduction of the risk of war and trust building as an integral part of relations among states.

I.

Our most important action is a concrete program aimed at the complete elimination of nuclear weapons throughout the world and covering a precisely defined period of time.

The Soviet Union is proposing a step-by-step and consistent

process of ridding the Earth of nuclear weapons, to be implemented and completed within the next fifteen years, before the end of the century.

The twentieth century has given humanity the gift of the energy of the atom. However, this great achievement of the human mind can turn into an instrument of the self-annihilation of the human race.

Is it possible to solve this contradiction? We are convinced it is. Finding effective ways toward eliminating nuclear weapons is a feasible task, provided it is tackled without delay.

The Soviet Union is proposing a program of ridding humankind of the fear of a nuclear catastrophe, to be carried out beginning in 1986. And the fact that this year has been proclaimed by the United Nations the International Year of Peace provides an additional political and moral incentive for this. What is required here is rising above national selfishness, tactical calculations, differences and disputes, whose significance is nothing compared to the preservation of what is most valuable— peace and a safe future. The energy of the atom should be placed at the exclusive service of peace, a goal that our socialist state has invariably advocated and continues to pursue.

It was our country that as early as 1946 was the first to raise the question of prohibiting the production and use of atomic weapons and to make atomic energy serve peaceful purposes for the benefit of humanity.

How does the Soviet Union envisage today in practical terms the process of reducing nuclear weapons, both delivery vehicles and warheads, leading to their complete elimination? Our proposals can be summarized as follows.

Stage One. Within the next five to eight years the USSR and the USA will reduce by one half the nuclear arms that can reach each other's territory. On the remaining delivery vehicles of this kind each side will retain no more than 6,000 warheads.

It stands to reason that such a reduction is possible only if the USSR and the USA mutually renounce the development, testing and deployment of space strike weapons. As the Soviet Union has repeatedly warned, the development of space strike weapons will dash the hopes for a reduction of nuclear weapons on Earth.

The first stage will include the adoption and implementation of the decision on the complete elimination of intermediate-range missiles of the USSR and the USA in the European zone, both ballistic and cruise missiles, as a first step toward ridding the European continent of nuclear weapons.

At the same time the United States should undertake not to transfer its strategic and medium-range missiles to other countries, while Great Britain and France should pledge not to build up their respective nuclear arms.

The USSR and the USA should from the very beginning agree to stop any nuclear explosions, and call upon other states to join in such a moratorium as soon as possible.

We propose that the first stage of nuclear disarmament should concern the Soviet Union and the United States because it is up to them to set an example for the other nuclear powers to follow. We said that very frankly to President Reagan of the United States during our meeting in Geneva.

Stage Two. At this stage, which should start no later than 1990 and last for five to seven years, the other nuclear powers will begin to engage in nuclear disarmament. To begin with, they would pledge to freeze all their nuclear arms and not to have them in the territories of other countries.

In this period the USSR and the USA will go on with the reductions agreed upon during the first stage and also carry out further measures designed to eliminate their medium-range nuclear weapons and freeze their tactical nuclear systems.

Following the completion by the USSR and the USA of the fifty per cent reduction in their relevant arms at the second stage, another radical step is taken: All nuclear powers eliminate their tactical nuclear arms, namely the weapons having a range (or radius of action) of up to 1,000 kilometers. At the same stage the Soviet-American accord on the prohibition of space strike weapons would have to become multilateral, with the mandatory participation of major industrial powers in it.

All nuclear powers would stop nuclear-weapons tests.

There would be a ban on the development of nonnuclear weapons based on new physical principles, whose destructive capacity is close to that of nuclear arms or other weapons of mass destruction.

Stage Three will begin no later than 1995. At this stage the elimination of all remaining nuclear weapons will be completed. By the end of 1999 there will be no nuclear weapons on Earth. A universal accord will be drawn up that such weapons should never again come into being.

We have in mind that special procedures will be worked out for the destruction of nuclear weapons as well as the dismantling, re-equipment or destruction of delivery vehicles. In the process, agreement will be reached on the numbers of weapons to be destroyed at each stage, the sites of their destruction, and so on.

Verification with regard to the weapons that are destroyed or limited would be carried out both by national technical means and through on-site inspections. The USSR is ready to reach agreement on any other additional verification measures.

The adoption of the nuclear disarmament program that we propose would undoubtedly have a favorable impact on the negotiations conducted at bilateral and multilateral forums. The program would identify specific routes and reference points, establish a specific time frame for achieving agreements and implementing them and would make the negotiations purposeful and goal oriented. This would break the dangerous trend whereby the momentum of the arms race is greater than the progress of negotiations.

In summary, we propose that we should enter the Third Millennium without nuclear weapons, on the basis of mutually acceptable and strictly verifiable agreements. If the United States Administration is indeed committed to the goal of the complete elimination of nuclear weapons everywhere, as it has repeatedly stated, it is being offered a practical opportunity to begin this in practice. Instead of wasting the next ten to fifteen years by developing new, extremely dangerous weapons in space, allegedly designed to make nuclear arms useless, would it not be more sensible to start eliminating those arms and finally bring them down to zero? The Soviet Union, I repeat, proposes precisely that.

The Soviet Union calls upon all peoples and states and, naturally, above all nuclear states, to support the program of eliminating nuclear weapons before the year 2000. It is absolutely clear to any unbiased person that if such a program is implemented, nobody would lose and everybody stands to gain. This is a problem common to all mankind and it can and must be solved only through common efforts. And the sooner this program is translated into practical deeds, the safer life will be on our planet.

II.

Guided by the same approach and the desire to make another practical step within the context of the program of nuclear disarmament, the Soviet Union has taken an important decision.

We are extending by three months our unilateral moratorium on any nuclear explosions, which expired on December 31, 1985. Such a moratorium will remain in effect even longer if the United States for its part also stops nuclear tests. We propose once again to the United States to join this initiative, whose significance is evident to practically everyone in the world.

It is clear that adopting such a decision was by no means simple for us. The Soviet Union cannot display unilateral restraint with regard to nuclear tests indefinitely. But the stakes are too high and the responsibility too great for us not to try every possibility of influencing the position of others through the force of example.

All experts, scientists, politicians and military men agree that the cessation of tests would indeed block off the channels for upgrading nuclear weapons. And this task has top priority. A reduction of nuclear arsenals alone, without a prohibition of nuclear-weapons tests, does not offer a way out of the dilemma of nuclear danger, since the remaining weapons would be modernized and there would still remain the possibility of developing increasingly sophisticated and lethal nuclear weapons and evaluating their new types at test ranges.

Therefore, the cessation of tests is a practical step toward eliminating nuclear weapons.

I wish to say the following from the outset. Possible references to verification as an obstacle to the establishment of a moratorium on nuclear explosions would be totally groundless. We declare unequivocally that verification is no problem, so far as we are concerned. Should the United States agree to stop all nuclear explosions on a reciprocal basis, appropriate verification of compliance with the moratorium would be fully ensured by national technical means as well as through international procedures—including on-site inspections whenever necessary. We invite the United States to reach agreement to this effect.

The USSR is strongly in favor of the moratorium becoming a bilateral, and later a multilateral action. We are also in favor of resuming the trilateral negotiations involving the USSR, the USA and Great Britain on the complete and general prohibition of nuclear-weapons tests. This could be done immediately, even this month. We are also prepared to begin without delay multilateral test ban negotiations within the framework of the Geneva Conference on Disarmament, with all nuclear powers taking part.

Nonaligned countries are proposing consultations with a view to making the 1963 Moscow Treaty banning nuclear-weapons tests in the atmosphere, in outer space and underwater apply also to the underground tests, which are not covered by the Treaty. The Soviet Union is agreeable to this measure too.

Since last summer we have been calling upon the United States to follow our example and stop nuclear explosions. Washington has as yet not done that despite the protests and demands of public opinion, and contrary to the will of most states in the world. By continuing to set off nuclear explosions, the U.S. side continues to pursue its elusive dream of military superiority. This policy is futile and dangerous, a policy which is not worthy of the level of civilization that modern society has reached.

In the absence of a positive response from the United States, the Soviet side had every right to resume nuclear tests starting already on January 1, 1986. If one were to follow the usual "logic" of the arms race, that, presumably, would have been the thing to do.

But the point is that it is precisely that notorious logic that has to be resolutely repudiated. We are making yet another attempt in this direction. Otherwise the process of military rivalry will become an avalanche and any control over the course of events would be impossible. To submit to the force of the nuclear arms race is inadmissible. This would mean acting against the voice of reason and the human instinct of self-preservation. What is required are new and bold approaches, a new political thinking and a heightened sense of responsibility for the destinies of the peoples of the world.

The U.S. Administration is once again given more time to weigh our proposals on stopping nuclear explosions and to give a positive answer to them. It is precisely this kind of response that people everywhere in the world will expect from Washington.

The Soviet Union is addressing an appeal to the United States President and Congress, to the American people. There is an opportunity for halting the process of upgrading nuclear arms and developing new weapons of that kind. It must not be missed. The Soviet proposals place the USSR and the United States in an equal position. These proposals do not attempt to outwit or outsmart the other side. We are proposing to take the road of sensible and responsible decisions.

III.

In order to implement the program of reducing and eliminating nuclear arsenals, the entire existing system of negotiations has to be set in motion and the highest possible efficiency of disarmament machinery ensured.

In a few days the Soviet-American talks on nuclear and space arms will resume in Geneva. When we met with President Reagan last November in Geneva, we had a frank discussion on the whole range of problems that constitute the subject of those negotiations, namely on space, strategic offensive arms and in-

termediate-range nuclear systems. It was agreed that the negotiations should be accelerated and that agreement must not remain a mere declaration.

The Soviet delegation in Geneva will be instructed to act in
strict compliance with that agreement. We expect the same
constructive approach from the U.S. side, above all on the question of space. Space must remain peaceful. Strike weapons
should not be deployed there. Neither should they be developed.
And let there also be a most rigorous control, including opening
the relevant laboratories for inspection.

Humanity is at a crucial stage of the new space age. And it
is time to abandon the thinking of the Stone Age, when the chief
concern was to have a bigger stick or a heavier stone. We are
against weapons in space. Our material and intellectual capabilities make it possible for the Soviet Union to develop any weapon
if we are compelled to do this. But we are fully aware of our
responsibility to the present and future generations. It is our
profound conviction that we should approach the Third Millennium not with the "Star Wars" program but with large-scale
projects of peaceful exploration of space by all humankind. We
propose to start practical work on such projects and their implementation. This is one of the major ways of ensuring progress on
our entire planet and establishing a reliable system of security
for all.

To prevent the arms race from extending into space means
to remove the obstacle to deep cuts in nuclear weapons. There is
on the negotiating table in Geneva a Soviet proposal on reducing
by one half the relevant nuclear arms of the Soviet Union and
the United States, which would be an important step toward a
complete elimination of nuclear weapons. Barring the possibility
of resolving the problem of space means not wanting to stop the
arms race on Earth. This should be stated in clear and straightforward terms. It is not by chance that the proponents of the
nuclear arms race are also ardent supporters of the "Star Wars"
program. These are the two sides of the same policy, hostile to
the interests of people.

Let me turn to the European aspect of the nuclear problem.

It is a matter of extreme concern that in defiance of reason and contrary to the national interests of the European peoples, American first-strike missiles continue to be deployed in certain West European countries. This problem has been under discussion for many years now. Meanwhile, the security situation in Europe continues to deteriorate.

It is time to put an end to this course of events and cut this Gordian knot. The Soviet Union has for a long time been proposing that Europe should be freed from both intermediate-range and tactical nuclear weapons. This proposal remains valid. As a first radical step in this direction we are now proposing, as I have said, that even at the first stage of our program all intermediate-range ballistic and cruise missiles of the USSR and the USA in the European zone should be eliminated.

Achieving tangible practical results at the Geneva talks would give meaningful material substance to the program designed to totally eliminate nuclear arms by the year 2000, which we are proposing.

IV.

The Soviet Union considers as fully feasible the task of completely eliminating, even in this century, such barbaric weapons of mass destruction as chemical weapons.

At the talks on chemical weapons within the framework of the Geneva conference on disarmament certain signs of progress have recently appeared. However, these talks have been unreasonably protracted. We are in favor of intensifying the talks in order to conclude an effective and verifiable international convention prohibiting chemical weapons and destroying the existing stockpiles of those weapons, as agreed with President Reagan at Geneva.

In the matter of banning chemical weapons, just as in other disarmament matters, all participants in the talks should take a fresh look at things. I would like to make it perfectly clear that the Soviet Union is in favor of an early and complete elimination of those weapons and of the industrial base for their production.

We are prepared for a timely declaration of the location of enterprises producing chemical weapons and for the cessation of their production and ready to start developing procedures for destroying the relevant industrial base and to proceed, soon after the convention enters into force, to eliminating the stockpiles of chemical weapons. All these measures would be carried out under strict control, including international on-site inspections.

A radical solution to this problem would also be facilitated by certain interim steps. For example, agreement could be achieved on a multilateral basis not to transfer chemical weapons to anyone and not to deploy them in the territories of other states. As for the Soviet Union, it has always strictly abided by those principles in its practical policies. We call upon other states to follow that example and show equal restraint.

V.

Along with eliminating weapons of mass destruction from the arsenals of states, the Soviet Union is proposing that conventional weapons and armed forces become subject to agreed reductions.

Reaching agreement at the Vienna negotiations could signal the beginning of progress in this direction. Today it would seem that a framework is emerging for a possible decision to reduce Soviet and U.S. troops and subsequently freeze the level of armed forces of the opposing sides in Central Europe. The Soviet Union and our Warsaw Treaty allies are determined to achieve success at the Vienna Talks. If the other side also wants this, 1986 could become a landmark for the Vienna Talks too. We proceed from the understanding that a possible agreement on troop reduction would naturally require reasonable verification. We are prepared for it.

As for observing the commitment to freeze the number of troops, in addition to national technical means permanent verification posts could be established to monitor any military contingents entering the reduction zone.

Let me now mention such an important forum as the Stockholm Conference on Confidence and Security-Building Measures and Disarmament in Europe. It is called upon to place barriers against the use of force or covert preparations for war, whether on land, at sea or in the air. The possibilities have now become evident.

In our view, especially in the current situation, it is essential to reduce the number of troops participating in major military maneuvers notifiable under the Helsinki Final Act.

It is time to begin dealing effectively with the problem still outstanding at the conference. It is known that the bottleneck there is the issue of notifications regarding major ground force, naval and air force exercises. Of course, those are serious problems and they must be addressed in a serious manner in the interests of building confidence in Europe. However, if their comprehensive solution cannot be achieved at this time, why not explore ways for their partial solution? For instance, reach agreement now about notifications of major ground force and air force exercises, postponing the question of naval activities until the next stage of the conference.

It is not an accident that the new Soviet initiatives in considerable part are directly addressed to Europe. In achieving a radical turn toward the policy of peace, Europe could have a special mission. That mission is erecting a new edifice of détente.

For this Europe has a necessary historical experience, which is often unique. Suffice it to recall that the joint efforts of the Europeans, the United States and Canada produced the Helsinki Final Act. If there is a need for a specific and vivid example of new thinking and political psychology in approaching the problems of peace, cooperation and international trust, that historic document could in many ways serve as such an example.

VI.

Ensuring security in Asia is of vital importance to the Soviet Union, which is a major Asian power. The Soviet pro-

gram for eliminating nuclear and chemical weapons by the end
of the current century is in harmony with the sentiments of the
peoples of the Asian continent, for whom the problems of peace
and security are no less urgent than for the peoples of Europe. In
this context one cannot fail to recall that Japan and its cities
Hiroshima and Nagasaki became the victims of nuclear bomb-
ing and Vietnam a target of chemical weapons.

We highly appreciate the constructive initiatives put forward by the Socialist countries of Asia and by India and other
members of the nonaligned movement. We view as very important the fact that the two Asian nuclear powers, the USSR and
the People's Republic of China, have both undertaken not to be
the first to use nuclear weapons.

The implementation of our program would fundamentally
change the situation in Asia, rid the nations in that part of the
globe, too, of the fear of nuclear and chemical warfare, and
bring the security in that region to a qualitatively new level.

We regard our program as a contribution to a search, together with all Asian countries, for an overall comprehensive
approach to establishing a system of secure and durable peace
on this continent.

VII.

Our new proposals are addressed to the whole world. Initiating active steps to halt the arms race and reduce weapons is a
necessary prerequisite for coping with the increasingly acute
global problems: Those of deteriorating human environment and
of the need to find new energy sources and combat economic
backwardness, hunger and disease. The pattern imposed by militarism—arms instead of development—must be replaced by the
reverse order of things—disarmament for development. The
noose of the trillion-dollar foreign debt, which is now strangling
dozens of countries and entire continents, is a direct consequence of the arms race. The over two hundred and fifty billion
dollars annually siphoned out of the developing countries is an
amount practically equal to the size of the mammoth U.S.

military budget. Indeed, this coincidence is far from accidental.

The Soviet Union wants each measure limiting and reducing arms and each step toward eliminating nuclear weapons not only to bring nations greater security but also to make it possible to allocate more funds for improving people's lives. It is natural that the peoples seeking to put an end to backwardness and achieve the level of industrially developed countries associate the prospects of freeing themselves from the imperialist burden of foreign debt, which is draining their economies, with limiting and eliminating weapons, reducing military expenditures and switching resources to the goals of social and economic development. This theme will undoubtedly figure most prominently at the international conference on disarmament and development to be held next summer in Paris.

The Soviet Union is opposed to making the implementation of disarmament measures dependent on the so-called regional conflicts. Behind this dependency is both the unwillingness to follow the path of disarmament and the desire to impose upon sovereign nations what is alien to them and what would make it possible to maintain profoundly unfair conditions, whereby some countries live at the expense of others, exploiting their natural, human and spiritual resources for the selfish imperial purposes of certain states or aggressive alliances. The Soviet Union, as before, will continue to oppose this. It will continue consistently to advocate freedom for the world's peoples, peace, security, and a stronger international legal order. The Soviet Union's goal is not to whip up regional conflicts but to eliminate them through collective efforts on a just basis, and the sooner the better.

Today, there is no shortage of statements professing commitment to peace. What is really in short supply is concrete action to strengthen its foundations. All too often peaceful words conceal war preparations and power politics. Moreover, some statements made from high rostrums are in fact intended to eliminate any trace of that new "spirit of Geneva" which is having a salutary effect on international relations today. It is not only a matter of statements. There are also actions clearly designed to incite animosity and mistrust and to revive confrontation which is antithetical to détente.

We reject such a way of acting and thinking. We want 1986 to be not just a peaceful year but one that would enable us to reach the end of the twentieth century under the sign of peace and nuclear disarmament. The set of new foreign policy initiatives that we are proposing is intended to make it possible for humanity to approach the year 2000 under peaceful skies and with peaceful space, without fear of nuclear, chemical or any other threat of annihilation and fully confident of its own survival and of the continuation of the human race.

The new resolute measures now taken by the Soviet Union for the sake of peace and of improving the overall international situation give expression to the substance and the spirit of our internal and foreign policies and their organic unity. They reflect the fundamental historic law which was emphasized by Vladimir Ilyich Lenin. The whole world sees that our country is holding even higher the banner of peace, freedom and humanism raised over our planet by the Great October Revolution.

On the questions of preserving peace and saving humanity from the threat of nuclear war, no one should remain indifferent or stand aloof. This concerns all and everyone. Each state, large or small, socialist or capitalist, has an important contribution to make. Every responsible political party, every social organization and every person can also make an important contribution.

No task is more urgent, more noble and humane, than uniting all efforts to achieve this lofty goal. This task is to be accomplished by our generation without shifting it onto the shoulders of those who will succeed us. This is the imperative of our time. This, I would say, is the burden of historic responsibility for our decisions and actions in the time remaining until the beginning of the Third Millennium.

The course of peace and disarmament will continue to be pivotal to the foreign policy of the CPSU and the Soviet state. In actively pursuing this course, the Soviet Union is prepared to engage in wide-ranging cooperation with all those who stand on positions of reason, good will and an awareness of responsibility for assuring the human race a future without wars or weapons.

3

A JOINT
SOVIET–AMERICAN
STATEMENT

BY MUTUAL agreement, General Secretary of the CPSU Central Committee Mikhail Gorbachev and President of the United States Ronald Reagan met in Geneva on November 19-21, 1985. Attending the meeting on the Soviet side were member of the Politburo of the CPSU Central Committee and Foreign Minister of the USSR Eduard Shevardnadze; First Deputy Foreign Minister of the USSR Georgy Kornienko; the USSR Ambassador to the United States Anatoly Dobrynin; head of the Propaganda Department of the CPSU Central Committee Alexander Yakovlev; head of the International Information Department of the CPSU Central Committee Leonid Zamyatin; Assistant to the General Secretary of the CPSU Central Committee Andrei Alexandrov. Attending on the American side were U.S. Secretary of State George Shultz; the White House Chief of Staff Donald Regan; Assistant to the President for National Security Affairs Robert McFarlane; U.S. Ambassador to the USSR Arthur Hartman; Special Advisor to the President and the Secretary of State for Arms Control Paul H. Nitze; Assistant Secretary of State for European Affairs Rozanne Ridgway; Special Assistant to the President for National Security Affairs Jack Matlock.

These comprehensive discussions covered the basic questions of Soviet-U.S. relations and the current international situation. The meetings were frank and useful. Serious differences remain on a number of critical issues.

While acknowledging the differences in the sociopolitical systems of the USSR and the USA and their approaches to international issues, some greater understanding of each side's view was achieved by the two leaders. They agreed about the need to improve U.S.-Soviet relations and the international situation as a whole. In this connection the two sides have confirmed the importance of an ongoing dialogue, reflecting their strong desire to seek common ground on existing problems.

The General Secretary of the CPSU Central Committee and the President of the United States agreed to meet again in the nearest future. The President of the United States accepted an invitation by the General Secretary of the Central Committee of the CPSU to visit the Soviet Union and the General Secretary accepted an invitation by the President of the United States to visit the United States of America. Arrangements for and timing of the visits will be agreed upon through diplomatic channels.

At their meetings, agreement was reached on a number of specific issues. Areas of agreement are registered below.

I.

The sides, having discussed key security issues, and conscious of the special responsibility of the USSR and the U.S. for maintaining peace, have agreed that a nuclear war cannot be won and must never be fought. Recognizing that any conflict between the USSR and the U.S. could have catastrophic consequences, they emphasized the importance of preventing any war between them, whether nuclear or conventional. They will not seek to achieve military superiority.

The General Secretary and the President discussed the negotiations on nuclear and space arms.

They agreed to accelerate the work at these negotiations, with a view to accomplishing the tasks set down in the joint Soviet-U.S. agreement of January 8, 1985, namely to prevent an arms race in space and to terminate it on Earth, to limit and reduce nuclear arms and enhance strategic stability.

Noting the proposals recently advanced by the Soviet Union and the U.S., they called for early progress, in particular in areas where there is common ground, including the principle of fifty per cent reductions in the nuclear arms of the U.S. and the USSR appropriately applied, as well as the idea of an interim agreement on medium-range missiles in Europe. During the negotiation of these agreements, effective measures for verification of compliance with obligations assumed will be agreed upon.

The sides agreed to study the question at the expert level of centers to reduce nuclear risk, taking into account the issues and developments in the Geneva negotiations. They took satisfaction in such recent steps in this direction as the modernization of the Soviet-U.S. hotline.

General Secretary Gorbachev and President Reagan reaffirmed the commitment of the USSR and the U.S. to the Treaty on the Nonproliferation of Nuclear Weapons and their interest in strengthening, together with other countries, the nonproliferation regime and in further enhancing the effectiveness of the treaty, *inter alia*, by enlarging its membership.

They note with satisfaction the overall positive results of the recent review conference of the Treaty on the Nonproliferation of Nuclear Weapons.

The USSR and the U.S. reaffirm their commitment, assumed by them under the Treaty on the Nonproliferation of Nuclear Weapons, to pursue negotiations in good faith on matters of nuclear arms limitation and disarmament in accordance with Article VI of the Treaty.

The two sides plan to continue to promote the strengthening of the International Atomic Energy Agency and to support the activities of the agency in implementing safeguards as well as in promoting the peaceful uses of nuclear energy. They view positively the practice of regular Soviet-U.S. consultations on nonproliferation of nuclear weapons which have been businesslike and constructive and express their intent to continue this practice in the future.

In the context of discussing security problems, the two sides reaffirmed that they are in favor of a general and complete prohibition of chemical weapons and the destruction of existing stockpiles of such weapons. They agreed to accelerate efforts to conclude an effective and verifiable international convention on this matter.

The two sides agreed to intensify bilateral discussions on the level of experts on all aspects of such a chemical weapons ban, including the question of verification. They agreed to initiate a dialogue on preventing the proliferation of chemical weapons. The two sides emphasized the importance they attach to the Vienna negotiations on the mutual reduction of armed forces and armaments in Central Europe and expressed their willingness to work for positive results there.

Attaching great importance to the Stockholm Conference on Confidence and Security-Building Measures and Disarmament in Europe and noting the progress made there, the two sides stated their intention to facilitate, together with the other participating states, an early and successful completion of the work of the conference. To this end, they reaffirmed the need for a document which would include mutually acceptable confidence and security-building measures and give concrete expression and effect to the principle of nonuse of force.

II.

General Secretary Gorbachev and President Reagan agreed on the need to place dialogue on a regular basis and intensify it at various levels. Along with meetings between the leaders of the two countries, this envisages regular meetings between the USSR Minister of Foreign Affairs and the U.S. Secretary of State, as well as between the heads of other ministries and agencies. They agreed that the recent visits of the heads of ministries and departments in such fields as agriculture, housing and protection of the environment have been useful.

Recognizing that exchanges of views on regional issues, including those on the expert level, have proven useful, they agreed to continue such exchanges on a regular basis.

The sides intend to expand the programs of bilateral cultural, educational and scientific-technical exchanges, and also to develop trade and economic ties. The General Secretary of the Central Committee of the CPSU and the President of the United States attended the signing of the agreement on contacts and exchanges in scientific, educational and cultural fields.

They believe that there should be greater understanding

among our peoples and that to this end they will encourage greater travel and people-to-people contact.

They agree that matters concerning individual citizens should be resolved in the spirit of cooperation.

The two leaders also noted with satisfaction that, in cooperation with the government of Japan, the Soviet Union and the United States have agreed to a set of measures to promote safety on air routes in the North Pacific and have worked out steps to implement them.

They acknowledged that delegations from the Soviet Union and the United States have begun negotiations aimed at resumption of air services. The two leaders expressed their desire to reach a mutually beneficial agreement at an early date. In this regard, an agreement was reached on the simultaneous opening of consulates-general in New York and Kiev.

Both sides agreed to contribute to the preservation of the environment—a global task—through joint research and practical measures. In accordance with the existing Soviet-U.S. agreement in this area, consultations will be held next year in Moscow and Washington on specific programs of cooperation.

The two leaders agreed on the utility of broadening exchanges and contacts including some of their new forms in a number of scientific, educational, medical and sports fields (*inter alia*, cooperation in the development of educational exchanges and software for elementary and secondary school instruction; measures to promote Russian language studies in the United States and English language studies in the USSR; the annual exchange of professors to conduct special courses in history, culture and economics at the relevant departments of Soviet and American institutions of higher education; mutual allocation of scholarships for the best students in the natural sciences, technology, social sciences and humanities for the period of an academic year; holding regular meets in various sports and increased television coverage of sports events). The two sides agreed to resume cooperation in combatting cancer diseases.

The relevant agencies in each of the countries are being

instructed to develop specific programs for these exchanges. The resulting programs will be reviewed by the leaders at their next meeting.

The two leaders emphasized the potential importance of the work aimed at utilizing controlled thermonuclear fusion for peaceful purposes and, in this connection, advocated the widest practicable development of international cooperation in obtaining this source of energy, which is essentially inexhaustible, for the benefit of all mankind.

November 21, 1985

4

PRESS CONFERENCE
IN GENEVA

Mikhail Gorbachev, General Secretary of the Central Committee of the Communist Party of the Soviet Union, held a press conference for journalists covering the Soviet-American meeting at the Soviet Press Center in Geneva on November 21, 1985.

OUR TALKS with the President of the United States of America, the first in the past six and a half years, have just ended. This has been, beyond a doubt, a significant event in international life. The importance of this meeting will become even more obvious if one considers not only Soviet-American but international relations in general, which are experiencing a special, I would say, difficult, period.

First, a few words about what had preceded the Geneva meeting. It had been awaited with impatience all over the world. People linked with it their great hopes for an improvement of the world situation and a lowering of international tension, which has reached a danger point. True, there were some doubts: Hasn't the confrontation of the two powers gone too far for counting on any accords at all? All that was there, you know it as well as we do.

As far as the Soviet side, the Soviet Union, is concerned, we fully realized the actual situation and did not nourish the slightest illusion regarding American policy. We saw how far the militarization of the economy and even the political thinking in that country had gone.

But we also understood that the situation in the world is too dangerous to neglect even the slightest chance of setting things right and moving toward a more stable and secure peace.

Well in advance of the meeting, within months of it, we had begun to sort of pave the way to it and create a propitious climate for this meeting. Back in the summer we unilaterally suspended all nuclear explosions, expressing our readiness to immediately resume the talks about a general nuclear test ban. We also reaffirmed our unilateral moratorium on the testing of anti-satellite weapons and, as you know, put forward radical proposals for a reduction of nuclear arsenals. Our proposals to prevent the arms race from spreading into space were accompanied by proposals for starting the broadest possible international cooperation in the peaceful exploration and use of space for the good of all nations.

I repeat, even before the meeting, we were doing everything so as to lay the groundwork for mutual understanding and make the political atmosphere healthier. In the period leading up to the Geneva summit, the Political Consultative Committee of the Warsaw Treaty member states held a session in Sofia which heard the socialist nations speak out for peace, détente and cooperation, for an improvement of the international situation in the interests of all peoples of the Earth, and against the arms race and confrontation.

And although our moves, prompted by a sense of responsibility for the fortunes of peace, fetched no proper response from our partners in the talks to be held in Geneva, we stood firm by a constructive position. We found it necessary to try and reverse the dangerous course of events by the force of arguments, the force of example, the force of common sense. The very complexity of the international situation convinced us that a direct conversation with the U.S. President was necessary. Because of the tremendous role that both the Soviet Union and the United States of America play, these states and their political leaders naturally have just as tremendous a responsibility to bear. Our conclusion was this: The time has come to learn the great art of living together in the face of a nuclear danger to all. Both the Soviet people and, I think, the American people, are equally interested in learning this art. This is something that all of the world's peoples are interested in.

We have always felt that people in all countries aspire to peace, and not only want peace to be preserved but the situation to be improved and real progress to be made in the struggle to halt the arms race. This desire is growing stronger and this is a fact of tremendous importance. Two major conclusions can be drawn from it.

On the one hand, it is an encouraging fact that everything we do meets the hopes and aspirations of a vast number of people in the world, regardless of where they live and whatever their political views, religious persuasions and traditions. On the other hand, this fact not only encourages us but imposes many duties on us, and a special responsibility.

What characterizes the present stage of development of the international situation? In a nutshell, it is growing responsibility for the future of the world. The peoples have realized this tremendous responsibility, and they are doing everything they can to live up to it.

This means that states and political leaders should be guided by these characteristics in their practical policies. The absence of a policy adequate to the needs of the moment, needs which are felt by all the peoples of the world, cannot be replaced by all sorts of propaganda wrappings. The people have quickly learned to see what is what and put everything in its proper place.

This is my profound conviction. This is how my colleagues in the political leadership of the Soviet Union and I understand the situation, and we have therefore focused our attention on a constructive search for a better and more tranquil world.

I was greatly impressed by the letters I received from the Soviet Union, the United States, Australia, Europe, Asia and Africa. They were from children, women, men, war veterans. I would like to emphasize that in those letters I could clearly hear the voice of the world's youth, those to whom the future belongs, who are just making a start in life and assuming upon themselves responsibility for the world's future.

Now about the meeting itself.

It was largely a private meeting with President Reagan. When the U.S. President and I were saying goodbye to each other a short while ago, we decided to count the number of confidential meetings we had had. We decided that there were five or six. Most of our meetings lasted for an hour, some a little longer. This is not simple arithmetic. Our discussions were straightforward, lengthy, sharp and at times very sharp. Nevertheless, I think they were productive to some extent. Of course, they took a great deal more time than planned: They occupied most of the time of these two days.

This allowed us to discuss a broad range of problems while looking into each other's eyes. We spoke political language, open and straightforward, and I think that was the most important thing.

These discussions and also the plenary sessions and broad contacts between all members of the delegations and experts at appropriate levels—these were internationally known authorities on both the Soviet and American sides—made it possible to accomplish in two days a tremendous amount of work.

We acquainted the President with our views and assessment of the situation in the world. The point of reference in our analysis is as follows: During the past few decades dramatic changes have taken place in the world which require a new approach and a new assessment of many things in foreign policy. There is a very important thing about the international situation today which we and the United States must take into account in our foreign policy. What I mean is this. Today it is not only a matter of confrontation of the two social systems but of a choice between survival and mutual destruction.

In other words, the objective course of world affairs has placed the problem of war and peace and the problem of survival in the center of world politics. I would like to emphasize that I am using the word "survival" not because I want to dramatize the situation or escalate fear but because I want all of us to feel deeply and realize the realities of the modern world.

The problem of war and peace is a problem of paramount importance, a burning problem of concern to all of us living on this planet. I would like to emphasize that this problem is now in the center of world politics. We must not avoid looking for a solution to this crucial problem. This is our firm belief. This is the will of the Soviet people. This is also the will of the American people and of all the peoples of the world. This is what I wanted to say in the first place.

Second, we once again drew the attention of the American side to the following factors of which I have already spoken. These factors are so important, and we attach such serious attention to them that we deemed it necessary to mention this again in Geneva—namely, it is a fact that it is already very difficult for us to commence a productive dialogue and talks on questions relating to stopping the arms race and nuclear disarmament. It will be even more difficult to do so tomorrow.

That is why it was necessary to hold a meeting, a responsible dialogue. All of us have come up to a point at which it is necessary to stop, to have a look around, to think better of it and to decide, on the basis of realities, on the basis of a wide approach to determining national interests, what is to be done in the world in the future. In the course of the meetings and talks I wanted to comprehend the stand of the present U.S. Administration on this cardinal issue—the question of war and peace.

All of us have read a lot on this score. Generally speaking, you journalists have also said quite a lot about this. But for the decision-makers it is essential to understand the starting point for the shaping of the partners' policy, the initial design of the foreign policy of the present U.S. Administration. It took a lot of work, a lot of effort to appraise everything objectively, with great responsibility and with a broad outlook, and to find an answer to this very important question.

This analysis has shown that, despite all the differences in the sides' approaches and appraisals which came into the open during this serious and necessary job—it was impossible to go to the summit without having done this job—it seems to me we saw that we have elements in common that can serve as the starting point for improvement in Soviet-U.S. relations. I mean the understanding of the fact that a nuclear war is inadmissible, that it cannot be waged and is unwinnable. This idea was voiced more than once both by us and by the American side. It is only logical to conclude from this that the problem of security is the central issue in relations between our countries at the present stage. We emphatically stand for achieving agreements ensuring equal security for both countries.

We are aware that consistent strengthening of mutual trust and general improvement of the political atmosphere, in which one could hope for the development of a political dialogue, for a fruitful discussion of the economic and humanitarian problems and the problems of contacts and reciprocal information, will become possible exactly on this basis. Herein lies the key to the problem of preserving life on Earth, to changing the political atmosphere toward one of goodwill.

We told the President that we did not and would not seek to gain military superiority over the USA. Furthermore, I repeatedly tried, both tête-à-tête and at the plenary meetings, to express our profound conviction that a lower level of security for the United States of America compared with that of the Soviet Union would not benefit us because this would lead to mistrust and generate instability. We are counting on an analogous approach by the USA to the questions relating to our country. At the same time, we told the President that we would never allow the USA to gain military superiority over us. In my view, this is a logical formulation of the question. Both sides had better get accustomed to strategic parity as a natural state of Soviet-U.S. relations. What we should discuss is how to lower the level of this parity through joint efforts, i.e. ways to carry out real measures to reduce nuclear armaments on a mutual basis. This is a field of action worthy of the leaders of such great states as the Soviet Union and the United States of America, as well as leaders of other states, because it is an issue of concern to all of us.

But this perfectly logically leads up to the following conclusion of fundamental importance. Neither of us, the United States of America nor the Soviet Union, should do anything that might open the door for the arms race in new spheres, specifically, in space. If the door into space is opened for weapons, the scope of military confrontation would grow immeasurably and the arms race would acquire an irreversible character, which to a certain extent can be predicted even now, getting totally out of control. In that case each side would all the time have the feeling that it has fallen behind in something, so it would be frantically looking for ever new countermoves. All this would spur on the arms race, not only in space but on Earth, too, for such countermoves should not necessarily be taken in the same sphere. They just have to be effective.

I use the same line of reasoning now as I did talking to the President. If such a situation does arise, I repeat that the possibility of agreement on any restraint upon military rivalry and the arms race will grow extremely problematic. I would like to return to the point which I have already made: The distinctive feature of the present situation is that we have come to a certain brink. So unless the existing problems are considered and thought out with genuine responsibility, wrong conclusions by politicians may lead to such steps which will have the most dire consequences for all nations.

Of course, neither the differences between our countries nor our rivalry will disappear, but we must do everything so that this does not overstep reasonable bounds and lead to military confrontation. Let each of the two social systems prove its advantages through example.

We have a good idea of not only the weak but also the strong aspects of American society and of other advanced nations. We are aware of their accomplishments and their potential. And, of course, we know our own potential even better, including those aspects of it which still require materialization. In other words, we are for competition with the U.S. and, I might add, for active competition. It is history itself rather than mere theoretical reckoning and speculations that has confirmed the viability of the policy of peaceful coexistence.

Much in the development of relations between the USSR and the U.S. depends on the way each side apprehends the surrounding world. We think that here it is particularly important to have a clear understanding of the historical realities and to take them into account in policy-making. I refer here both to the Soviet and to the American leadership.

Today's world is a highly diversified assembly of sovereign states, of nations with their own interests, aspirations, policies, traditions and dreams. Many of them have just embarked on the road of independent development. Their first steps come in the impossibly difficult conditions left over from the days of colonialism and foreign domination. Some of them, having gained political sovereignty, are seeking now to obtain economic independence. They see that they have the resources and the manpower, or the things which, given the adequate time to work through, can secure a better life for them. Why, these are whole great continents. So it is only natural that each nation should seek to exercise its sovereign rights in the political, economic and social fields.

One may like or dislike this policy, but it does reflect the inner processes in each particular country and the interests of each given nation which possesses that sovereign right. This is the right to choose the way, the system, the methods, the forms and the friends. This right belongs to each nation. I don't know how international relations can possibly be built without the recognition of this right.

When I was in Great Britain last December, I recalled a phrase by Palmerston. It had settled in my memory when I was studying international relations in the law department of Moscow State University. Palmerston said that Britain had no eternal enemies or eternal friends, but only eternal interests. I told Margaret Thatcher then that I agreed with that judgement. But if Palmerston and you, the present political leader of Britain, admit that you do have such interests, you must admit that the other nations and other countries have interests of their own.

When about two hundred states are involved in the international arena, each of them strives to promote its own interests. But to what extent are these interests promoted? It depends on taking into account the interests of others in the course of cooperation. But to look upon the world as somebody's private domain is an approach which we renounce. We have always said so—10 years ago and today, and we will be saying so tomorrow. We have no dual policy here. We pursue an honest and frank policy. We have been doing so, we shall continue to do so.

The causes of tension, conflicts in some regions, even wars between various states in one or another part of the world are found both in the past and in the present socioeconomic conditions of those countries and regions. To present the whole thing as if those contradictory knots have been born of the rivalry between East and West is not only erroneous but also extremely dangerous. I said this to the President and to the American delegation.

If today, for example, Mexico, Brazil and several other

states fail to pay not only their debts but also interest on those debts, one can imagine what processes are taking place in those countries. This may strain the situation and lead to an explosion. Will they again be talking about the "hand" of Moscow? But one simply cannot subject the whole world to such judgements on these issues in so irresponsible a manner. These banalities can still be found somewhere, but they are inadmissible, particularly at such meetings as the one we are having. That is why we said right away: Let us not tell each other banalities, for a lot of these were uttered on the eve of and in the course of preparations for the meeting. It was a real skirmish that proceeded, not without the help of you journalists. (Animation in the hall.)

Of course, the Soviet Union and the United States are two mighty powers with their own global interests and with their own allies and friends. They have their priorities in their foreign policies. Yet the Soviet leadership regards it not as a source of confrontation but rather as the origin of a special, greater responsibility for the destiny of peace shouldered by the Soviet Union and the United States and their leaders. This is how we see it. Of course, we can argue about the situation in one or another part of the world. Our conclusions may be different, often contradictory, particularly when the matter concerns any particular event and the causes of any particular conflicts. In principle, we are not against discussing any particular regional problems to find ways promoting their settlement. We discussed them and agreed with the President to continue to exert joint efforts, something that has been reflected in the final Joint Statement. Yet we always emphasize—and I want to say it now again—we are against any kind of interference in the internal affairs of other states. Such is our conception of Soviet-American relations which we brought to the meeting and presented to the President and the American delegation. It was presented in a more detailed manner, but I have just tried to convey its essence to you.

We believe that improvement of Soviet-U.S. relations is quite possible. Many problems have accumulated, I would say, whole obstructions that should be cleared away. Soviet leaders have the political will to tackle this job. But it should be done jointly with the American side. It is known that when geologists and miners come up against cave-ins and find themselves in a critical situation, rescue teams converge to save people.

In order to save our relations from being further strained, to prevent them from moving toward confrontation and to turn them toward a normal course, toward improvement, this work should be done through joint efforts. We are ready for this. I told the U.S. President that it would be a big mistake if we fail to use the chance that has presented itself for changing the situation in Soviet-U.S. relations toward normalization, and this means toward improvement of the situation in the world as a whole.

I would like to return again to the main issue which was pivotal to the Geneva meeting, as it were. There was not a single meeting of the delegations, not a single confidential meeting, where questions of war and peace and arms control did not hold a central place. These were the pivot of the Geneva meeting. We explained to the U.S. side that the "Star Wars" program would not merely give an impulse to the arms race involving weapons of all types, but that it would also put an end to any restrictions on the arms race. In reply, we were told again and again that the large-scale antimissile system with space-based elements was allegedly defensive in character. We were asked: What would you tell the Soviet people after Geneva if you refused to effect a reduction in offensive arms? We gave an answer to that, and I repeat it: This isn't so. We are prepared for a sweeping reduction in nuclear arms providing the door is firmly closed on starting an arms race in space. On that condition, we are ready to cover the first stage on the basis of the principle of a 50 per cent reduction in nuclear arms and then, drawing the other nuclear powers into this process, to move further on the road of radical reduction.

There is a certain part of the world, and perhaps there are even some politicians and journalists, who have a positive reaction, so to speak, to the SDI. It is alleged that this is a weapon of defense, a shield. This is absolutely not so. As a matter of fact, although mountains of weapons have been stockpiled in the world, the arms race is under way and we cannot for all our efforts cope with this process, put it under control, curb or reverse it. In this highly complicated situation the United States proposes that we start a race in space. Who could guarantee that we would then be able to organize any effective talks? I think no man in his right mind would guarantee this. The American side is reluctant to admit that the SDI means bringing weapons to space. Weapons. They would fly over people's heads in waves— American and Soviet weapons. We would all watch this sky and expect something to fall from there. We told the American side—let us imagine the consequences of even an accidental collision in space. Say, something has become separated from a missile, the nose part has gone off on its own and the vehicle has broken away to collide with a space weapon subsystem. There would be signals which could be interpreted as perhaps an attempt by the other side—I don't even say which side, ours or theirs—to destroy these weapons. All computers would be switched on while politicians would not be able to do anything sensible. Shall we allow such things to prevail over us? We can imagine many such situations. I told the U.S. President: We understand that this idea has captivated him as a man and we can understand this to some extent or another. However, what we cannot understand in this respect is his position as a politician responsible for such a mighty state, for security matters. We think that after the talks we had the American side will weigh in earnest everything we said on this score.

The meeting has shown once again that the Americans do not like our logic, while we cannot find logic in their arguments. They say: Believe us, if the Americans were the first to deploy the SDI, they would share their experience with the Soviet Union. I then said: Mr. President, I call on you to believe us. We have said that we would not be the first to use nuclear weapons and we would not attack the United States. Why then do you, while preserving the defense capability on Earth and underwater, intend to start the arms race also in space? You don't believe us? This shows that you don't. Why should we believe you more than you believe us? Especially since we have reasons not to believe you, since we invite you to leave space in peace and start disarmament on Earth. All this is comprehensible to everybody.

In general, it is to be hoped this is not all the American side has to say. The talk with the President was serious. We attentively listened to each other's arguments and recorded all these things. If the United States found the will and resolution to give the matter new thought and evaluate all the pernicious aspects and implications of the "Star Wars" program, this would give the go-ahead to the effective handling of the international security issue and ending the arms race. In saying this, I mean that this refers to control matters as well. There is a lot of speculation around this issue, with the Soviet stand being deliberately misrepresented. However, the truth is that the Soviet Union is open for verification. Provided an accord is reached to ban deploying weapons in space, we are prepared to open our laboratories, on a reciprocal basis, in order to monitor such an agreement. However, what has been proposed looks like this: Let us open our laboratories and monitor the progress of the arms race in space. It's naive and, besides, the premise is wrong and unacceptable.

If the American side also stopped all tests of nuclear weapons and we signed a relevant agreement, there would be no problems with control, including international verification, on our side of this issue too.

If both sides agree to cut their nuclear weapons by 50 per cent, then of course it will be necessary to verify this process, and we are interested in this no less than the Americans.

I want to say just a few words to the effect that at this stage differences have been revealed in the positions with regard to the 50 per cent cut in nuclear weapons. We have our reservations concerning the draft submitted by the American side, and the Americans have theirs with regard to our drafts. But we do not dramatize these differences and are ready to seek a mutually acceptable solution if of course an arms race in space is not started. The proposals of the two sides are a foundation for seeking mutually acceptable solutions. There can be compromises here. This will require time and clarification of the situation. We are prepared to look for these solutions proceeding from the basic principle that we are not striving to achieve military superiority and that we stand for equal security.

There was an exchange of views on humanitarian problems at the meeting. This has resulted in corresponding agreements reflected in the Joint Statement. I'll remind you that understanding has been reached on some questions of bilateral Soviet-American relations and on extending contacts in science, culture, education and information. An exchange of students, TV programs and sports delegations will be broader. An understanding in principle has been reached on concluding an agreement on air links. I think that information has already come from Moscow that it seems this problem too was removed yesterday.

I would like to draw your special attention to the fact that it has been decided to jointly appeal to a number of states concerning cooperation in the field of thermonuclear synthesis. This is a very interesting idea. Its realization can turn a new page in a very important sphere—providing a practically inexhaustible source of energy to humankind. This is an area for joint activity. This calls for tremendous efforts on the part of scientists, for tremendous efforts of experts and for new solutions. All this will advance technological progress and technology.

I think that from the point of view of the political results and consequences of the Summit, it is important to take one more factor into account. We have witnessed the great political effect of the meeting. It has shown and heightened the world public's interest in the problems of Soviet-American relations, in the danger of the arms race and in the necessity of normalizing the situation.

I have to mention several episodes in this connection. The day before yesterday a group of the leaders of U.S. peace movements, led by prominent politician Jesse Jackson, visited our mission. I want to say that we have always regarded them as worthy and respected American citizens representing the millions of people living in the USA who have signed a message to President Reagan and to me with wishes for the success of the meeting and with specific proposals aimed at strengthening peace, including the call to stop nuclear tests. The American World War II veterans who participated in the Elbe Linkup came to Geneva, and representatives of many mass organizations of other countries, children's organizations included, were also here these last few days. At my request, they were received by the Soviet delegation. It was a moving meeting. It is needless to say here that we constantly felt the powerful support and solidarity of our socialist friends and of the nonaligned countries. Even before the Summit the leaders of six states—India, Mexico, Argentina, Tanzania, Greece and Sweden—introduced a proposal to freeze all types of nuclear weapons. We highly appreciate their initiative. A large group of Nobel Prize winners advanced proposals all of which, save one, I was ready to support right away. That wish, or demand, was that we should not leave Geneva until we have reached an accord. It was risky to agree to this. Otherwise, it might have taken us too long before we could go home. (Animation among the audience.) At this moment I would have thought differently. I would have, most likely, supported this proposal, too. (Laughter and applause among the audience.)

Ladies and gentlemen, comrades,

It so happens at the sharp, crucial turns of history that moments of truth are as necessary as the breath of life. As a result of the intensifying arms race, the international situation has become too dangerous, and too many stories on this score are spun to scare people. It has really become necessary to dispel this fog and to test words by deeds. The best way to do this is to have a frank talk, that kind of talk which is presupposed by a summit meeting, especially considering our states' role and responsibility in the world. Issues are discussed here on a different plane, where it is no longer possible to try to evade the truth. So, when we speak about the general results of the meeting, any hard-and-fast appraisal would hardly be right. Of course, it would have been much better if in Geneva we had reached accord on the crucial, key issue—the problem of terminating the arms race. Regrettably, this has not happened.

For the time being, the American side has proved to be unprepared for major decisions. But I think that it was impossible to complete this process within two days anyway, even if it had taken such a course. We have a mechanism. But at the same time the meeting is too important an event to be appraised by any simplified standards. It has made it possible to get a better idea of the character of our differences, to remove—at least, I think and hope so—some of the biased ideas with regard to the USSR and to the policy of its leadership, and to get rid of part of the amassed prejudices. This may have a favorable effect on the further course of developments. It is impossible to restore trust at once. This is no easy process. We paid attention to the assurances by the American President that the USA does not seek military superiority and does not want a nuclear war. It is our sincere wish that these statements be confirmed by deeds.

We would like to regard the summit as the commencement of a dialogue with a view to effecting changes for the better both in Soviet-American relations and in the world in general. In this sense I would appraise the meeting as one creating opportunities for progress.

Such is, in general outline, our appraisal of the results and significance of the Geneva meeting. And this gives me ample reason to look into the future with optimism as I am leaving hospitable Geneva. Common sense must prevail. See you again! (Applause.)

*   *   *

Mikhail Gorbachev then answered journalists' questions.

Question: (BBC, Great Britain). Mr. General Secretary, in your opinion, what are the prospects for relations between the USSR and the USA and for the international situation as a whole after the Geneva meeting?

Answer: For the most part, I optimistically look to the future. If we all continue to act in the spirit of responsibility both in Soviet-American relations and in international relations as a whole, which was nevertheless felt at the Geneva meeting, we shall find answers to the most burning issues and approaches to their solution. I am deeply convinced of this.

Question: (Soviet Television). You have mentioned the

need for a new approach in international relations today, even for a new way of thinking. What do you regard as the essence of such a new approach, a new way of thinking?

Answer: Yes, I am convinced that at this stage in international relations, which is characterized by a greater interrelationship of states, by their interdependence, a new policy is required.

We feel that the new approach makes it incumbent that the realities of today's world should nourish current policy for any state. This is the most important prerequisite for the constructiveness of a state's foreign policy. This is what will lead to an improvement of the situation in the world.

The problem of war and peace is the focal point of world politics. It is a special concern of all nations.

All countries—developed capitalist, socialist and developing—have economic problems, social problems and ecological problems. These problems can be more successfully solved on the basis of cooperation and mutual understanding. It takes a dialogue, it calls for more cooperation, it takes a pooling of efforts.

Take the problems of the developing world. We cannot fence ourselves off from them. And the new policy, based on realities, obliges us all to look for answers to the problems of this multitude of states which are striving for a better life.

The most important point—and I return to it—is that everything should be done to stop the arms race. An awareness of this is growing. Unless this problem is solved, all our other hopes, plans and actions can be undermined.

I am convinced that with the old approach, based on purely egoistic interests—although this is presented as the defense of national interests—there will be no movement forward. A new policy is required that will correspond to the present stage, taking into account the realities pushed to the fore by the very course of world development.

Question: (NBC, USA). During World War II the United States and the Soviet Union fought together against fascism and defeated it. Considering your talks with President Reagan, do you think that the Soviet Union and the United States of America can again become allies in the struggle against hunger in Africa, against international terrorism, against the pollution of the environment, against such diseases as cancer?

Answer: I thank you for your recalling an important stage of our common history. We remember it, we do not forget it. I think that as a result of the Geneva meeting opportunities will open up for broad cooperation between our countries and peoples. And when I say between our countries and peoples, I do not oversimplify the situation.

I know the depth of the differences now separating us. I'm conscious of the real state of current Soviet-American relations. But I am convinced that cooperation is possible, including on the problems you mentioned. I do not want to dwell now on the nuances of these problems. We shall be able to release huge funds to come to the aid of the developing countries.

Today, in Latin America alone, an enormous number of people, half of them children, are starving or are undernourished. A reduction of world arms spending by just 5 to 10 per cent would make it possible to remove this problem.

So all this deserves our giving thought to this problem.

I welcome your question and answer it affirmatively, although this does not mean that there are not certain nuances here in approaching the problems you mentioned.

Question: (NBC television network, USA). You have said that you are disappointed with President Reagan's response regarding the SDI. There are as many weapons now, after the meeting, as before it. Can it be said that the world has become safer after the Geneva summit, and if so, why?

Answer: I would venture claiming that although the amount of weapons has remained unchanged since before the meeting, the world has grown safer. Anyway, it seems to me that the meeting itself and its results are a definite contribution to the cause of security, since the meeting constitutes the beginning of the road to dialogue and understanding, or to the things that work for the benefit of security. In this sense, Geneva has certainly produced such an effect.

Question: (Pravda). What concrete, practical steps could be undertaken by the Soviet Union and the United States to secure the earliest end to the arms race?

Answer: Although I have devoted all of my speech here to this subject, I will say again: We must stop.

If we keep the arms race out of space, both our proposals and those proposed by the American side will allow us to move ahead, to look for compromises and to seek parity at a lower level. There is a good mechanism for this: the Geneva talks.

I would also add that we hope that the U.S. Administration still has not had its final say concerning the prohibition of all nuclear-weapons tests. The whole world is for such a ban. There is still time for the American side to consider the situation. A positive decision would be a momentous step stimulating the termination and reduction of the arms race.

I think that further intensification of the political dialogue between the USSR and the United States of America will likewise contribute to this process. We have agreed to expand it, and I think that the participation of the top leaders of our countries in this political dialogue will be instrumental in curbing the arms race.

Here is another point. The things dealt with at the Geneva talks, or the objectives and the subject of these talks, are a cause of all nations. Responsible politicians and, first of all, the leaders of states must adopt a firm and constructive stand on this issue. That would be a move of colossal importance.

I think that the overwhelming majority of politicians are in favor of speeding up the search for solutions in Geneva and of finding ways to stop the arms race and to proceed to disarmament.

Question: (GDR Television). What are, in your opinion, the most important results of the meeting? And another question: What is the significance of top-level political dialogue?

Answer: To answer your question, I would first of all point out that the Geneva meeting is an important stage in Soviet-American relations. It lays the groundwork for the search for ways to improve and normalize them in all directions. If this search continues in the future joint efforts of the two sides, it will help improve the situation in the world. This is what I would call the political result.

At the Geneva meeting attention was focused on the issues which concern all nations of the world. The Joint Statement by the leaders of the Soviet Union and the United States saying that nuclear war is impossible, that it should never be started, that they are not seeking military superiority and that they will impart a fresh impetus to the Geneva talks—is of great importance in itself if it is consistenty implemented with practical moves.

Now the second question. I think that the meeting has shown that under any conditions the thing to be done is to try and maintain a political dialogue which helps compare mutual positions, to understand each other better and to look for mutually acceptable solutions to the most distressing problems of today's world on this basis.

Question: (The Italian newspaper *Il Mattino*). The Soviet Union suffered heavy material and human losses during the Second World War. This notwithstanding, don't you think that 40 years after the end of the war the Soviet Union could help with the unification of the two German states?

Answer: I think that this question was very thoroughly discussed and considered at the conference in Helsinki. The Helsinki process and the Final Act signed by all states of Europe, as well as by the USA and Canada, are our common achievement. The Helsinki process deserves being supported and developed in every way. That is why it is the results of the Helsinki Conference that provide an answer to your question.

Question: (Swiss Radio). You stressed the deep distinction in the stand of the USSR and the USA on "Star Wars." Will this not hamper progress at the Geneva talks?

Answer: I do not want to repeat what I have said before. Our stance can be expressed in a few words. We adhere to a constructive line at the Geneva negotiations. We shall do our best to come to decisions to stop the arms race and to effect a radical reduction of nuclear armaments so as to really achieve, at one of the subsequent stages, the elimination of nuclear weapons with the participation of all nuclear powers. It is our strong belief that this is possible if the door to an arms race in outer space is bricked up.

Question: (Associated Press). You spoke about the President's personal allegiance to the "Star Wars" program and said that you had discussed the SDI in detail. What was his attitude to your arguments? How did he react to them? Do you see any chance to get things moving in this field?

Answer: I think that after the meeting the American side has ample reason to think over everything we have said. We hope for understanding of our arguments. In our view, their logic is in line with the spirit of the January accord, namely, that as a result of the Geneva talks we must take the road of drastic reductions of nuclear armaments provided an arms race in space is prevented.

This objective was jointly determined by us earlier. The U.S. President states that the SDI is a shield. I hope that we have convincingly shown that it is a space weapon which can be used against missiles, against satellites and against targets on Earth. It is a new type of weapon. A new sphere of the arms race is thereby opened. This is unacceptable. This would complicate the whole situation and would make the atmosphere at the Geneva talks problematic.

That is why I appreciate the fact that it was stressed at the level of the U.S. President and the General Secretary of the CPSU Central Committee that the work at the negotiations in Geneva would be speeded up on the basis of the January accord.

Now it is already a point of view confirmed by the signatures of not only the ministers of foreign affairs but also of the leaders of the two states. We view this as a certain signal and hope.

Question: (BBC). If you do not succeed in coming to agreement on stopping the arms race in space, would the Soviet Union be able to compete with American technology in this field or will it fall behind?

Answer: You have touched on a very interesting subject. I

tried to explain to the President in a very open and straightforward talk that, as it seems to me, much in American policy in respect to the Soviet Union is built on delusions. On the one hand, some hope that the continued arms race will wear out the Soviet Union economically, weaken its influence in the world and so give the United States of America a free hand. History has put such prophets to shame. And that was at a time when our society had a different potential from what it has today and had smaller opportunities. Now we have immense potential, and delusions regarding us only stand in the way of a realistic policy.

On the other hand, there have been delusions in terms of military calculations. There was an attempt to outdo us. They phased in intercontinental ballistic missiles. Our response followed. A little later, but it did follow. Next came independently targetable nuclear warheads. The response followed. We always found the way to respond.

Now, as it seems to me, the illusions in the U.S. military establishment have affected, to some extent, political quarters, perhaps, the President, too. I do not maintain this, yet that is the impression we have formed.

Some people in the U.S. apparently believe that the Americans have a certain edge on us in some aspects of technology, computer technology and radioelectronics. Again there is a desire, seizing upon that edge, to secure military superiority. Once more some are quoting President Johnson, who once said that the nation that would dominate space would dominate the Earth as well. There are some people who have their fingers itching to obtain world supremacy and look down upon the world. Those are old ambitions of bygone years. The world has changed very much in many ways.

So, speaking of the so-called technological superiority that the SDI is supposed to bring with it and thus put the Soviet Union into an awkward predicament, I want to say that this is yet another delusion. We would find the way to respond.

That is just what I told the President. Please note that there are no simpletons here.

If the President is so much committed to the SDI, we,

understandably, consider it our duty to thoroughly analyze the "Star Wars" program.

And so we did. Especially since there has been a kind of invitation from the American side: Let us see, let us analyze it, let us talk not of how to prevent space from being militarized, but of what kind of weapon to take into space. We are against that. We are against an arms race in space.

We have looked into another aspect of the matter. Suppose, the Americans do not accept our arguments and do not appreciate our goodwill and our appeal to find a way to end the arms race and cut the available stocks of nuclear weapons, that is, if they continued to move in the same direction. We would, of course, find a way to respond.

The Soviet leadership gave appropriate instructions to competent organizations and scientists at one time, and we can say that our response would be effective, less expensive and could come within shorter time limits.

But that is not our political choice. Our choice is to prompt the U.S. to think over the entire situation, after all, and pursue a responsible policy based on common sense and the mood and aspirations of people rather than compound what is the most dramatic problem of international relations.

Question: (Czechoslovakian Television and the newspaper *Rude Pravo*). In what particular, practical fields do you perceive chances for developing Soviet-American relations after meeting with President Reagan?

Answer: I think the political dialogue will be furthered, and it will be conducted at various levels. We agreed to exchange visits, something that in itself must be welcomed. We will have more opportunities to promote bilateral cooperation in those spheres which we agreed upon. Apparently, we will continue and expand our consultations on regional problems and the situations in various parts of the world.

Finally, we proceed from a premise that both in our country and in the U.S. business community there is still a good deal of mutual interest—I know this for certain—in improving relations. If things go that way, the scope of economic cooperation may be expanded. We are prepared to invite U.S. businesses to take part in implementing some big projects. Our plans are vast. We are doing a lot to expand our cooperation with the Western Europeans. And we welcome it.

I conveyed to the President the idea that one cannot underestimate economic relations, and not just because they cannot do without us, or that we cannot do without the USA. We can do well without the USA, and, I hope, America can do well without us. But this is the material base for a political relationship, for its being made healthier, for enhancing the atmosphere of confidence.

Honestly speaking, economic ties engender mutual dependence. This mutual dependence is then reflected in the solutions to political problems. I think that it would be both to the advantage of the Soviet Union and the United States of America to continue furthering economic ties. But please don't think we are begging for this.

Question: (The Lebanese newspaper *Al Nahar Arab Report*). Did you discuss the situation in the Middle East, above all, that in Lebanon while speaking about regional problems? What is your forecast for the situation there after the Summit?

Answer: During the meeting we dealt with the situation in such regions as Central America, the Middle East and Africa. However, most of the time was devoted to discussing the principled aspects of these issues. We agreed to continue political consultations and expand the scope of cooperation in dealing with regional problems.

Question: (Soviet author Yulian Semyonov). Mikhail Sergeyevich, you have spoken about the need to learn the art of living together. My experience as an author tells me that since the sad times of McCarthy, the films and television of the United States have unfortunately been portraying the Soviet people to the American people as something like monsters. Don't you think that after the Geneva meeting it would be very important if in the USA they abandoned that kind of biased thinking and looked in a more impartial manner upon the Soviet people, as partners of the American people?

Answer: Here is what I am going to tell you, Comrade Semyonov. Don't you try to make political leaders shoulder all the burdens. (Animation in the hall.) We agreed to further cultural contacts—which include films—so please meet them and negotiate with them. One must act in the spirit of Geneva, meaning work for an improvement in Soviet-American relations.

5

A REPORT
TO THE USSR SUPREME
SOVIET SESSION
ON THE RESULTS
OF THE GENEVA SUMMIT
AND THE INTERNATIONAL
SITUATION

COMRADE deputies,

Major questions of the domestic and foreign policies of the Soviet state have been submitted for discussion at the current session of the USSR Supreme Soviet.

The laws on the state economic and social development plan of the USSR and on the state budget for 1986, passed by this session, are extremely important to our country, to its present and future, to every work collective, to every Soviet family. The new year, 1986, ushers in not merely the first year of the Twelfth Five-Year Plan period but a qualitatively new stage in the development of Soviet society.

The 1986 plan reflects the strategic policy of the Party toward accelerating the country's socioeconomic development. It provides for higher rates of growth of the national income, industrial and agricultural production, and labor productivity. Efficiency in the use of material resources will increase. Priority is given to developing the branches that are called upon to ensure scientific and technical progress and improve the quality of products.

Measures have been set forth for speeding up the reconstruction, refurbishing and modernization of production that will perfect management and the economic mechanism. A further rise in the people's well-being is envisaged.

It is important, Comrades, that all of us constantly take into account the specific features of the plan for 1986.

An even pace for all five years should be set as early as the first year of the five-year plan period. Proceeding from this, rates for developing the national economy for 1986 have been envisaged so that their implementation, as intensity gradually grows in subsequent years, will facilitate the implementation of assignments for the five-year period on the whole. This will help avoid the situation that occurred during the previous five-year period when reduced targets were fixed for the first years, while the major increment was planned for the final years. The negative results that this practice brought about are known.

The second specific feature of the plan is that it was shaped with the greatest consideration for the need to speed up scientific and technical progress. Proceeding from the directive of the June conference at the CPSU Central Committee, the plan includes, on a top-priority basis, assignments to accelerate the scientific and technical progress envisaged by resolutions on developing major directions in science and technology in branches of the national economy. Simultaneously, established principles in planning were largely revised. For the first time, the plan provides for generalized key indicators of the effectiveness of scientific and technical progress in the branches of the economy. These indicators are put in place with a view toward invigorating the practical work of ministries, amalgamations and enterprises, and toward ensuring advancement to the top levels of scientific and technical development.

The next specific feature of the 1986 plan is its orientation toward carrying out practical transfers to intensive methods of running the economy. This is dictated by life itself, by the complex situation of labor and material resources, and by the near exhaustion of extensive factors of economic growth. Next year, we are to achieve production growth through a maximum saving of resources. In other words, saving is actually becoming the main means of providing resources for the entire increment of production. Here are some figures that illustrate the point. Next year, 97 per cent of production growth will be gained through raised labor productivity. Metal consumption in the national income will drop by 2.7 per cent, and energy consumption will fall by three per cent.

And finally, an extensive transition to new methods of management has proved to be positive. Starting from January 1986, more than half of products manufactured by industry will be at enterprises working under the new conditions.

In general, Comrades, the policy is correct. Now we are to make it material—both in the process of further detailed elaboration of plans in the branches, republics, territories and regions, in amalgamations and enterprises, and, naturally, in concrete practical work. This aspect should be emphasized also because many workers in the center and in the provinces, including at planning and economic bodies, are not fully aware of the importance of assessing and resolving in a new way the country's economic, social and financial problems.

The current session is held at a crucial period immediately preceding the Party congress. The April Plenary Meeting of the Central Committee of the CPSU charted the course toward accelerating the social and economic development of society, marked the beginning of substantive changes in approaching the fulfillment of economic and political tasks, and set a new rhythm for all the work of Party, state and local government bodies and all our cadres and workers' collectives.

The Party's political course, both in domestic matters and international problems, has found its fullest reflection in the theoretical and political documents of paramount importance that will be submitted for consideration to the Twenty-seventh Congress of the CPSU. These are the draft of the new edition of the CPSU program, the proposed changes in the Party rules, and the Draft Guidelines for the Economic and Social Development of the USSR for 1986-1990 and in the Period till the Year 2000.

The Party is determined to be responsive to the people, and the first results of vast discussions show that the documents submitted for consideration evoke the profound satisfaction of the Soviet people. Our optimism, our confidence that the chosen road is correct and that what has been planned will certainly be fulfilled stems from the vigorous support for the Party's strategic course, supported by word and deed.

As you know, comrade deputies, the Central Committee of the Party and the Soviet Government have undertaken of late a number of important measures aimed at speeding up the switching of the economy toward intensive development and enhancing the efficiency of the management of the national economy. Further practical measures are being taken toward putting things in order, strengthening labor and state discipline, enforcing strict economy and combatting drunkenness and alcoholism.

In other words, vast, intensive work has been started in all spheres of public life, and it is beginning to bear fruit.

The new factors that are introduced into our life have now stirred up the Soviet people, boosted their creativity and showed once again the vastness of the resources and possibilities inherent in the socialist system.

We can now say with certainty that things have begun to look up. The growth rate of production is rising and other economic indicators are improving. Despite setbacks in a number of sectors of the national economy at the start of the year, the Soviet people managed to put the situation right and to ensure the fulfillment of economic plan targets. Change for the better is taking place in the agrarian sector of the country as well.

Immense credit for what has been achieved goes to our heroic working class, which sparing neither effort nor energy and overcoming difficulties has done everything possible to meet the plan targets. The positive results achieved are representative of the strenuous work of the collective farmers and all the other workers in the agroindustrial complex. Our achievements embody the creative thought of scientists, engineers and the people's intelligentsia. Soviet young people, who boldly and energetically come to grips with difficult and complex tasks and vigorously support the ongoing changes in our society, linking to it their own future, have pioneered and initiated many important undertakings.

We also associate these changes with the activization of the work of the Party, government and trade union bodies, and of all our cadres.

In short, comrade deputies, a good deal is being done. However, it would be an error to overestimate all this—and it is not our custom anyway. We are at the start of the road we have planned, the road which is arduous and difficult and which calls for a combination of a creative approach to the tasks posed by practice with a purposefulness and a high sense of discipline and dedication. We have immense reserves and opportunities and we must work hard to tap them and to use them to maximum benefit. This is to be done in every area of economic and cultural development, primarily in those in which the situation remains complex and which are slow to catch up and gain momentum.

Now that the current five-year period is drawing to a close, one should work hard so that we may start the next year with a confident and dynamic advance, ensure that the targets planned will be reached, and create the prerequisites for a further qualitative transformation of the country's productive forces.

Comrades, the plan for 1986 shows patently the peaceful, constructive nature of our concerns. Our foreign policy aspirations, the international policy of the Soviet state, are closely linked with this peaceful trend of domestic policy.

The foreign policy guidelines of the April Plenary Meeting of the CPSU Central Committee have become a concrete manifestation of Leninist foreign policy at the present stage. The plenary meeting has emphasized the need to intensify to the utmost the Soviet Union's peaceful policy on the broadest front of international relations. It has called for doing everything to ensure that the forces of militarism and aggression shall not prevail. It has emphasized the urgency of ending the arms race, of stepping up the process of disarmament, declared for the development of equal, proper, civilized relations between states and for the widening and strengthening of mutually-advantageous economic ties.

The directives of the plenary meeting were dictated by the times, the specificities of the situation and the demands of the socialist policy of peace and progress. In its assessment the Politburo of the CPSU Central Committee proceeded from the premise that the degree of the unpredictability of events grows as a result of the continuing arms race. The possibility of the militarization of outer space signifies a qualitatively new leap in the arms race. It would inevitably result in the disappearance of the very notion of strategic stability—the basis for the preservation of peace in the nuclear age. A situation would develop in which fundamentally new decisions, irreversible in their consequences, would in fact be taken by computers without the participation of the human mind and of political will, without taking into account the criteria of ethics and morality. Such a development of events could result in a universal catastrophe—even if the initial impulse were given by an error, miscalculation, or technical malfunctioning of sophisticated computer systems.

In other words, the development of world events has approached the point when especially responsible decisions are required, when lack of action or delay is criminal: For the point at issue today is the preservation of civilization and life itself. That is why we have believed and continue to believe that all necessary measures should be taken to break the vicious circle of the arms race, so as not to miss a single chance of reversing the course of events for the better. The question today is acute and definite in the extreme: It is necessary to rise above narrow interests, to realize the collective responsibility of all states in the face of the danger that looms over the human race at the threshold of the Third Millennium.

The April Plenary Meeting of the CPSU has instructed us to take precisely this line in the implementation of our foreign policy. This line is fully in keeping with the interests of the Soviet people and the peoples of socialist states. And, as we have become convinced, it has met with understanding in other countries. During a brief period of time marked by important international events, the Soviet Union has striven to interact in the interests of peace with a great number of states. We have been and are proceeding from the view that the period of dangerous tension can be ended only by the efforts of all countries, big and small.

Political and economic ties with countries of the socialist community have been intensified and deepened considerably in the past months. Long-term programs of cooperation in the sphere of economy and scientific and technical progress have been drawn up. A mechanism for effective, concrete ties has been created. Coordination of foreign policy activity has become more intensive. The meetings of the leaders of fraternal countries in Moscow, Warsaw, Sofia and Prague have become important milestones on the road of the further rallying of the socialist community. Ties with all the socialist countries develop and strengthen.

Cooperation with states that have gotten rid of colonial oppression, that participate in the nonaligned movement, assumes a broader nature. Important steps have been taken in the development of relations with many of those countries. This is a factor of great importance in the turbulent ocean of present-day international relations, a factor that operates in favor of peace, equality, freedom and the independence of peoples.

The Soviet Union is making an effort to improve ties with capitalist states as well. I will single out the recent Soviet-French summit in Paris, in the course of which substantial steps were undertaken toward the further development of bilateral cooperation, consolidation of European and international security and return to détente.

We will continue to build our foreign policy on a multiple foundation, on the basis of firm and stable bilateral relations with all countries. But the reality of today's world is such that there are states which—due to their military, economic, scientific and technical potential, and international position—bear a special responsibility for the character of world development, its course and consequences. It is primarily the Soviet Union and the United States which have this responsibility, I stress responsibility—not privilege.

Looking at things from this position, the Soviet-American summit held last week is, as the Politburo of the Central Committee of the CPSU assesses, an important event—not only in our bilateral relations, but in world politics on the whole. I have already shared my first impressions of the talks with the U.S. President at the press conference in Geneva. The meeting's final document—the Joint Statement—is known too.

Today, speaking at the session of the USSR Supreme Soviet, I would like to appraise the results and significance of the Geneva meeting in the context of the present-day situation, with due account taken for past experience and prospects for the future and for the tasks that we have to tackle.

First of all I must say that the road to the Geneva dialogue was long and arduous for many reasons. The U.S. Administration, which came to office in the early 1980s, openly assumed a course of confrontation while rejecting the very possibility of a positive development of Soviet-American relations. I think everyone remembers even today the pitch of anti-Soviet rhetoric of those years and the power politics practiced by the U.S. ruling circles.

The mutual efforts over many years to achieve the essential minimum of trust in those relations were committed to oblivion, and virtually every thread of bilateral cooperation was snapped. Détente itself was branded as being contrary to the interests of the United States of America.

Having assumed a course for reaching military superiority over the USSR, the Administration went ahead with programs for nuclear and other rearmament of the USA. U.S. first-strike missiles began to be deployed in Western Europe. In this way a situation was taking shape that was fraught with high-level military and political uncertainties and concomitant risks.

Lastly, there appeared a "Star Wars" program, the so-called "Strategic Defense Initiative." They in Washington became obsessed with it without giving much thought to those grave consequences which were bound to ensue if this idea were translated into practice. The plan to introduce weapons in outer space is extremely dangerous to all the peoples of the world, to all without exception.

But we knew something else as well: Such U.S. policies would inevitably clash with reality. And it happened. The Soviet Union together with its allies unequivocally declared that they would not allow military superiority over themselves.

Confusion emerged even among U.S. allies in the face of Washington's apparent disregard for the interests of their security, and its readiness to bank all on the pursuit of the will-o'-the-wisp of military superiority. In the United States itself this course generated serious doubts. The proclamation of the "Star Wars" preparation plans sounded alarm bells throughout the world.

It was miscalculation on the part of those who thought that their line of confrontation would determine world development. I will add, perhaps, in this connection, that dreams of world domination are basically wrong—both in what concerns the objective and in what concerns the means. As with designs of perpetual motion motors born out of a lack of knowledge of the elementary laws of nature, so imperial claims grow out of notions about the world which are far removed from present-day reality.

While giving a firm rebuff to the U.S. line of disrupting military-strategic equilibrium, the Soviet Union advanced large-scale peace initiatives and displayed restraint and constructiveness in the approach to the key issues of peace and security.

Our initiatives, and there are quite a number of them, clearly showed what we are seeking to achieve in the world arena, what we are urging the United States and its allies to do. These actions by the USSR found the enthusiastic approval of the world public. They were highly valued by the governments of many countries.

Under the influence of these factors, Washington was compelled to maneuver. Signs of demonstrative peacefulness appeared in the U.S. Administration's statements. They were not backed by deeds, but their very appearance was symptomatic.

Early this year an agreement was reached, at our initiative, on new talks between the USSR and the United States, talks to encompass the entire complex of space and nuclear armaments in their interrelationship, and aimed at preventing an arms race in outer space and terminating it on Earth.

The atmosphere of Soviet-American relations, and to some extent the international behavior of the United States, started to undergo changes which in fact, naturally, had to be taken into account when considering the possibility of holding a summit meeting.

By adopting this decision, we firmly proceeded from the premise that central to the talks would be the questions that determine our relations and the world situation in general—security issues. At that, we took into account political and strategic realities in Europe and the world, the opinion of our friends and allies, the views of the governments and public circles of many countries and their persistent calls on the Soviet Union to do everything possible so that the summit meeting would be held. We understood how many hopes were pinned on the meeting all over the world, and we undertook concrete steps to improve the international climate and to make it more favorable for the meeting.

We have put forward concrete and radical proposals in the Geneva negotiations on nuclear and space arms. What is their substance?

We have first of all proposed prohibiting space strike arms completely. We did so because the beginning of an arms race in outer space, and even only the deployment in near-Earth space of antimissile systems, will not contribute to the security of any state. Hidden behind a space "shield," offensive nuclear systems will become even more dangerous.

The appearance of space strike arms could turn the present strategic balance into a strategic chaos, could cause the arms race to proceed feverishly in all directions, and could undercut one of the fundamental pillars of its limitation—the ABM Treaty. As a result, mistrust in relations between states will grow and security will diminish considerably.

Further, in the conditions of the complete prohibition of space strike weapons we have proposed halving all nuclear systems of the USSR and the U.S. capable of reaching each other's territory and limiting the total number of nuclear warheads on such systems belonging to either side by a ceiling of 6,000. These are radical reductions of thousands of nuclear warheads.

Such an approach is fully justified. It embraces all those systems which form the strategic correlation of forces. It also makes it possible to take due account of the nuclear threat which really exists with respect to either side, regardless of how and from where nuclear warheads can be delivered to a territory, whether by missile or plane, from one's own territory or the territory of one's allies.

We regard the reduction of nuclear systems of the USSR and the U.S. by 50 per cent as a beginning. We are prepared to go further, right down to the complete elimination of nuclear weapons—a process in which other states having nuclear weapons should, naturally enough, be involved too.

It does not take much to realize that the race in nuclear arms is a source of special concern to European nations. We understand well why this is so. Europe is overflowing with nuclear systems. The Soviet Union stands for completely removing nuclear weapons, both medium-range and tactical ones, from Europe. However, the U.S. and its NATO partners do not agree to that. Then we proposed to start at least with provisional decisions and then to work toward further reductions. We are convinced that our proposals accord with the hopes of European nations for lessening the nuclear threat and enhancing European security.

I would like to emphasize the principled aspect of the matter: In the three areas of the negotiations—space, strategic offensive arms and medium-range nuclear systems—we do not propose to the U.S. anything that would lessen its security. Moreover, our proposals make it possible to resolve such issues which the American side elevates to the rank of its "special concerns."

For example, much is said about the Soviet intercontinental ballistic missiles. Our proposals provide for a reduction of the number of such missiles and the limitation of the share of their warheads in the overall number of nuclear munitions. Or, here is another example. There has been quite an outcry in the West around the Soviet SS-20 missiles. We propose reducing them substantially in the context of solving the problem of nuclear medium-range weapons in Europe.

Britain and France's nuclear weapon systems are presented as a stumbling block. It is said that they cannot be discussed at the Soviet-American talks. Well, we are prepared to seek a solution to this, too. We propose to start a direct exchange of opinions with those countries about their nuclear arms.

The Soviet proposals are met with a broad and positive response in the world. They are backed by the prestige of the Warsaw Treaty member states, which unanimously supported our constructive stand. Joint statements of the leaders of six countries—Argentina, Mexico, Tanzania, India, Sweden and

Greece—are largely consonant with our approach. The Soviet initiative was received with approval and hope by communist and workers' parties, large public organizations of different countries and continents, scientists of world renown, prominent politicians and military leaders. It evoked the positive response of most of the parties of the Socialist International.

What is more, there were thousands of letters from Soviet and foreign citizens that were addressed to me on the eve of the Geneva meeting and during it. I wish to take the opportunity to express gratitude to their authors for their good wishes, for their advice and support, and for their profound and sincere concern over safeguarding peace.

The Americans advanced their counterproposals on the eve of the meeting. This was a positive fact in itself. One of our numerous initiatives evoked a favorable response.

A lot was written in the press about the essence of these counterproposals. I shall not repeat their contents. I shall only say that these are indeterminate and largely inequitable proposals. They are based on a one-sided approach and are clearly prompted by a striving for the military superiority of the United States and NATO as a whole.

But the main thing is that the United States' stand does not envisage a ban on the creation of space strike arms. Quite the contrary, it seeks to legalize their creation. The stand assumed by the U.S. side in the question of "Star Wars" is the main obstacle to agreement on arms control. And this is not only our opinion. The governments of France, Denmark, Norway, Greece, the Netherlands, Canada and Australia refused to take part in the so-called "Strategic Defense Initiative." On the eve of the Geneva meeting the United Nations General Assembly adopted a resolution urging the leaders of the USSR and the USA to work out effective agreements aimed at the prevention of an arms race in space and its termination on Earth. It is only the United States and some of its allies that deemed it possible not to support this clear call of the world community. A fact, as it is said, that needs no comment.

It should also be recalled, perhaps, that there were powerful political forces at work in the United States, doing whatever they could to thwart the meeting or at least to make it meaningless and to nullify its importance. I think such steps as the test of an ASAT system, the entrance of the battleship *Iowa* with long-range cruise missiles into the Baltic, the speedy deployment of Pershings in West Germany, the decision on the development of binary chemical weapons and, finally, the adoption of a new all-time record military budget are fresh in the memory of many people.

Moreover, the President was already on his way to Geneva when a letter from the U.S. Defense Secretary, pleading with him not to make any agreements with the Soviet Union which would reaffirm the treaties on the limitation of strategic offensive weapons and on antimissile defense systems, was made public. In other words, the Defense Secretary wanted the USA to have a completely free hand to act in every venue of the arms race on Earth and in space.

And indeed, was the Pentagon alone standing in the way? We did not overlook either the "mandate" given to the U.S. President by the forces of the American extreme right-wing represented by their ideological headquarters, the Heritage Foundation. The President was instructed to carry on the arms race, not to give the Soviet Union any opportunity to convert resources to socioeconomic development programs and to seek eventually to crowd the USSR out of international politics. Those gentlemen went so far as to formulate for the U.S. Administration the task of forcing us to alter our system, to revise our Constitution! These are familiar tunes, Comrades. We have heard all this on more than one occasion. In short, there were quite a few attacks.

Yet we decided in favor of meeting the U.S. President. We took that decision because we had no right to disregard even the slightest chance to reverse dangerous world developments. We took that decision in the awareness that if we failed to start a direct and frank discussion now, tomorrow it would be a hundred times more difficult, if at all possible.

It is beyond question that differences between us are immense. But the interrelationship and interdependence between us in the present-day world is similarly immense. The crucial times we are living through leave the leaders of the USSR and the USA, the peoples of the USSR and the USA, no alternative to learning the great art of living together.

During our first one-on-one conversation with the President—and those conversations featured prominently at the Geneva meeting—it was stated directly that the Soviet delegation had come to seek solutions to the most urgent problem in the area of international affairs, the problem of averting nuclear war and curbing the arms race. That, as I told the President, was the main meaning of our meeting and that was what would determine its results.

I must stress that the Geneva talks were sometimes very acute and, I would say, frank to the utmost. It was impossible either to hoodwink each other there or to get away with political or propaganda stereotypes—too much depends on the pivotal questions of war and peace.

The American side stubbornly insisted at the meeting on going ahead with the SDI program. We were told that the point was the development of purely defensive systems, which were not even weapons as such. We were also told that those systems would help to stabilize the situation and to get rid of nuclear weapons altogether. There was even the proposal that in some foreseeable future these systems would be "shared" with us and that the two sides should open the doors of their laboratories to each other.

We frankly told the President that we did not agree to these evaluations. We had thoroughly analyzed all those questions and our conclusion was unequivocal. Space weapons are not at all defensive. They can breed the dangerous illusion that it is possible to deliver a first nuclear strike from behind a space "shield" and to avert, or at least weaken, retaliation. And what are the guarantees that space weapons in themselves would not be used against targets on Earth? There is every indication that the U.S. space-based ABM system is being conceived precisely as a component of an integrated offensive complex rather than as a "shield."

Naturally, we cannot agree to the allegation that the programed space systems are not weapons altogether. Neither can we rely on the assurances that the United States will share with us what they will develop in that field.

So if the doors of the laboratories have to be opened, it is only to verify compliance with a ban on the development of space strike weapons but not to legalize these weapons.

We are told about a desire to remove the fear of missiles and to achieve the total elimination of nuclear weapons. This desire can only be welcomed and it is fully in accord with the goals of our policy. But it is far easier to eliminate these weapons without developing space strike systems. Why spend tens and hundreds of billions of dollars and pile up mountains of space weapons in addition to nuclear armaments? What is the point?

I asked the President if the American leadership believed in all seriousness that at a time when American space weapons were being developed we would reduce our strategic potential and help the United States with our own hands to weaken this potential. No hopes should be pinned on this. Quite the contrary will happen: To regain the balance, the Soviet Union will have to improve the efficiency and accuracy and to raise the yield of its weapons so as to neutralize, if necessary, the electronic space machinery of "Star Wars" that is being developed by the Americans.

And will the Americans feel more secure if our weapons in space will be added to the echelons of space weapons planned by Washington? Indeed, the USA cannot really hope to achieve a monopoly in outer space. At least, not seriously.

However, the American Administration is still tempted to try out the possibility of achieving military superiority. At present, too, by designing an arms race in outer space, they hope to surpass us in the field of electronics and computers. But we will find a response, just as it happened several times in the past. The response will be effective, sufficiently prompt and, perhaps, less costly than the American program. We put this idea across to the President.

I think that in order to achieve a real turn in our relations, which would meet the interests of the USSR, the United States and the interests of the peoples of the world, what is required are new approaches, a fresh look at many things and, what is most important, political will on the part of the leadership of the two countries. The USSR—and I emphasized that in Geneva—does not feel enmity toward the United States, and it respects the American people. We are not building our policy on the desire to infringe on the national interests of the United States. I will say more: We would not like, for instance, a change of the strategic balance in our favor. We would not like that because such a situation will enhance the suspicion of the other side, will enhance the instability of the overall situation.

Life is developing in such a way that both our countries will have to grow accustomed to strategic parity as a natural state. We will have to come to a joint understanding in which the level of arms of either side can be considered relatively sufficient from the point of view of its dependable defense. We are convinced that the level of such sufficiency is well below what the USSR and the United States actually have at the present time. And this means that tangible practical steps in arms limitation and reduction are quite possible. These are measures which will not diminish the security of the USSR and the U.S. or the overall strategic stability in the world. On the contrary, they will enhance them.

What can be said about other questions discussed at the meeting?

I will begin with the problem of regional conflicts. Both sides expressed concern over the continuing existence of such "trouble spots." It is easy to understand why. Such conflicts are a dangerous thing, especially in light of the threat of their escalation in this nuclear age.

However, it can be said that our approaches to their causes and ways for settling such conflicts are not simply different—they are diametrically opposite. The United States, which is used to thinking in terms of "spheres of interests," reduces these problems to East-West rivalry. But these days it is an anachronism, a relapse into imperial thinking, which denies the right of a majority of nations to think and take decisions independently.

The deep-lying causes of such conflicts are multifaceted—to an extent they are rooted in history, but mainly, in those social and economic conditions into which the emergent countries have been put. It is definitely not by chance that in discussing the problem of regional conflicts the U.S. does not mention the atrocities of apartheid in South Africa, the aggression staged by that country against its African neighbors, the wars fought by American puppets in Central America and Southeast Asia, Israel's banditry in the Middle East and many other things. Washington is trying to equate the legitimate governments of the states that follow the path of national liberation and social progress with counterrevolution.

It goes without saying that we could not accept such an interpretation of the situation. The President was told that we are for the recognition of the inalienable right of every people to freedom and independence, to an independent choice of their road. We wish this right not to be flouted by anyone. There should be no attempts at outside interference. Freedom, not tyranny, should prevail. We have been and remain on the side of peoples upholding their independence. This is our principled line.

The President touched upon the question of Afghanistan. It was confirmed again in this connection that the Soviet Union consistently declares for a political settlement of the situation around Afghanistan. We stand for friendly neighboring Afghanistan to be an independent nonaligned state, for establishing a practice of guaranteed noninterference in Afghanistan's affairs. The question of withdrawal of Soviet troops from that country will thus also be resolved. The Soviet Union and the Government of Afghanistan are wholly for this. And if anybody hinders an early resolution of that question, it is, above all, the United States, which is financing, backing and arming gangs of counterrevolutionaries and is frustrating efforts at the normalization of the situation in Afghanistan.

Matters of bilateral relations assumed an important place

at the talks. A certain invigoration that has started in this area of late has now been borne out with concrete agreements on exchanges and contacts in the sphere of science, education and culture and on the resumption of air services between the two countries.

The potential inherent in this will, naturally, be much easier to bring into play in full measure under conditions where security matters decisive for our mutual relations start being tackled. If we are to cooperate, this must be cooperation on an equal footing, without any discrimination and preliminary terms advanced, without attempts at interference in internal affairs of the other side. Our stand on this is firm and consistent.

How can the main results of the Geneva meeting be assessed?

The meeting was, undoubtedly, a significant event. It was direct, clear and concrete talk, and the possibility to compare positions was useful. Too many explosive, acute problems are heaped up, problems that needed to be considered in earnest in order to try to overcome the deadlock on them.

We appreciate personal contact established with the President of the United States. A dialogue of top leaders is always a moment of truth in relations between states. It is important that such a dialogue has been held. It is a stabilizing factor in itself in the present troubled times.

But we are realists and we must say outright that solution of the most important questions connected with an end to the arms race was not achieved at the meeting. The unwillingness of the U.S. leadership to give up the program of "Star Wars" has made it impossible to achieve in Geneva concrete arrangements on real disarmament, above all, on the cardinal problem of nuclear and space arms. The amount of arms stockpiled by both sides has not lessened as a result of the meeting. The arms race continues. This cannot but cause disappointment.

There remain major differences between the USSR and the United States on a number of other issues of principle concerning the situation in the world and developments in individual regions. But we are also far from belittling the significance of the Geneva Accords.

I will recall the most important of them. These are, above all, the common understanding, sealed in the Joint Statement, that a nuclear war cannot be won and must never be fought, and the pledge by the USSR and the United States to build their relations proceeding from this indisputable truth, and not to seek military superiority.

We believe that this understanding, jointly endorsed at the highest level, should actually underlie the foreign policy of the two states. Since it is acknowledged that a nuclear war, by its very nature, cannot help attain any rational end, therefore, the stronger the stimulus should be in favor of its prevention, the termination of the development and testing of weapons of mass annihilation and the complete elimination of the stockpiles of nuclear armaments. Still more, it is inadmissible to open new directions in the arms race. Of course, the Joint Statement is not a treaty, but it is a principled directive that commits the leaders of the two countries to much.

Further, the USSR and the United States clearly reaffirmed their pledge to facilitate in all ways the enhancement of the effectiveness of the nuclear nonproliferation regime and agreed on practical steps in this direction. This is of no little importance in the disquieting present-day international situation for maintaining world stability and diminishing the risk of nuclear wars.

The Joint Statement of the leaders of the two countries in favor of the universal and complete prohibition and elimination of such barbarous weapons of mass destruction as chemical weapons has basic importance. We express hope that the United States will observe that important understanding in practical politics as well.

The agreement of the leadership of the USSR and USA to contribute jointly with the other states participating in the Stockholm Conference to its early completion, with the adoption of a document which would include both concrete obligations on the nonuse of force and mutually acceptable confidence-building measures, goes far beyond the boundaries of Soviet-American relations.

It is only to be welcomed that the meeting produced a number of useful agreements in many areas on the development of bilateral cooperation between the USSR and the USA. I hope that they will provide a good base for increasing trust between our countries and peoples. Naturally, this will be so if a careful attitude is taken to all the achievements and if everything positive built into those achievements is developed, but not if artificial pretexts are made up to throw them overboard.

The importance of the agreement reached in Geneva to continue political contacts between the Soviet Union and the United States, including new meetings at the summit level, should be mentioned specifically.

To sum it all up, we have every right to say that the overall balance sheet of the Geneva meeting is positive.

Undoubtedly, the constructive and consistent policy of our country contributed in a decisive degree to the achievement of such an encouraging outcome. Simultaneously, it would be wrong not to say here also that the position of the American side at the meeting included certain elements of realism, which helped to resolve a number of questions.

Of course, the real importance of everything useful agreed upon in Geneva can only manifest itself in practical deeds. I want to state in this context that the Soviet Union for its part intends not to slow down the pace and to seek most resolutely and in the spirit of honest cooperation with the United States the folding up of the arms race and the overall improvement of the international situation. We hope that the USA will display a similar approach. Then, I am certain, the work done in Geneva will bear real fruit.

This is our evaluation of that event and its role in international relations. I can say with satisfaction that this evaluation is shared by our allies, the fraternal socialist countries, and is borne out with utmost clarity by a meeting of the leaders of the Warsaw Treaty member countries in Prague immediately upon the completion of the Soviet-American summit talks.

The participants in the Prague meeting stressed that the

situation, of course, remained difficult. Struggle for improving it is being carried on but conditions for that struggle have become better, as can already be stated today. The Geneva meeting is an important element of our long-term joint and closely coordinated efforts to ensure peace.

A natural question to ask is: What is to be done now in the light of the results of the Soviet-American dialogue in Geneva?

As I have already said, we attach much importance to the agreement reached in Geneva on new Soviet-American summit meetings. I want to stress that our approach to this question is not formal. What is important is not the mere fact of another meeting between the leaders of the two countries but its results. The peoples will expect a practical advance on the road mapped out in Geneva. It is precisely this that we will be seeking. We should already begin making preparations for the next Soviet-American summit meeting now, first and foremost in the area of practical politics.

Not to make it more difficult to achieve new agreements, both sides, we are convinced, should first and foremost refrain from actions subverting what was achieved in Geneva, refrain from actions which could block talks and detract from the existing constraints on the arms race. This calls, *inter alia*, for strict and honest compliance with the treaty on the limitation of ABM systems and also for the further mutual respect by the sides for the relevant provisions of the SALT II Treaty.

But the main thing, of course, is to create a possibility for actually ending the arms race and initiating practical reductions in the existing nuclear arms arsenals.

Is there such a possibility? It is our firm conviction that there is. True, at present there are differences on many points between our proposals and the American proposals on nuclear arms reductions. But we do not overdramatize this circumstance. Compromises are possible here and we are prepared to look for them.

Undoubtedly, given such a course of developments, questions of dependable verification, in which the Soviet Union has a direct interest, could be resolved. One cannot rely on promises here, especially since the case in point is disarmament and the country's defenses.

But to resolve all these questions, it is absolutely essential to slam the door shut through which weapons could get into space. Without this, radical reductions in nuclear armaments are impossible. I want to state this with utmost responsibility on behalf of the Soviet people and their supreme body of power.

Accord is possible if it respects the interests of both sides. The stubborn desire of the American side to go ahead with the development of space weapons can have only one result, the blocking of the possibility of ending the nuclear arms race. This outcome, naturally, could bitterly disappoint the peoples of the whole world, including, I am certain, the American people.

There is a real chance today to sharply lessen the threat of nuclear war and subsequently to remove altogether any possibility of such a war. It would be a fatal mistake to miss that chance. We hope that what was said about the SDI in Geneva was not the last word of the American side.

We have come to terms with President Reagan on instructing our delegations to the Geneva talks on nuclear and space arms to speed up negotiations, carrying them forward on the basis of the January agreement between the two countries. Thus, it was confirmed by both sides at the highest level that it is necessary to prevent an arms race in space, resolving this question in conjunction with the reduction of nuclear arms. This is what the Soviet Union will press for. This is what we call upon the United States to do. By honoring the pledge we have made jointly with practical actions, we will live up to the hopes of the peoples of the world.

As time goes on the question of terminating nuclear tests is becoming more and more acute. This is so primarily because with an agreement an end would be put to the development of new types of nuclear weapons and the modernization of existing types. Further, without testing, without renovation, the gradual process of the withering away of nuclear arsenals and the demise of nuclear weapons would begin. Lastly, it is so because it is impossible to permit nuclear blasts—and their number stands in the hundreds—to deface our beautiful planet and intensify concern over how the succeeding generations will live on it.

This is why the Soviet Union has announced a moratorium on all types of nuclear tests till January 1, 1986, and is ready to extend this moratorium, given reciprocity on the part of the United States. We expect the U.S. leadership to make a concrete and positive decision that would have a very favorable effect on the entire situation, would change it greatly and build up trust between our countries.

We have put this question to the American President in Geneva.

Silence was the answer we heard. Really, in essence there are no reasonable arguments against the prohibition of nuclear tests. Difficulties of verification are sometimes mentioned. But the Soviet Union clearly demonstrated the excellent possibility of exercising such verification with the help of national means. This year we registered an underground nuclear blast of a very low yield staged in the United States and unannounced by it. We are also ready to examine the possibility of establishing international control. In this context special attention should be devoted to the ideas formulated in the message of the leaders of six states who proposed to set up special stations on the territories of their countries to monitor the observance of a test ban agreement.

The entire world raises its voice in favor of terminating nuclear tests. Not so long ago the United Nations General Assembly passed a resolution calling for such a move. Only three countries—the U.S., Britain and France—voted against it. This is a deplorable move.

But there's still time. I think that the leaders of the United States and other nuclear powers will use the existing opportunity and, proceeding from the interests of peace, will show the necessary responsibility. I would like to remind them that our moratorium remains in effect, and we hope that the discussion of that issue at the session of the Supreme Soviet of the USSR will be regarded as an urgent call for a realistic and immediate prohibition of all nuclear tests.

On the whole the Soviet Union is coming up with an all-embracing complex of measures which completely blocks all avenues for the arms race, be it in space or on Earth, be it nuclear, chemical or conventional weapons. Concrete proposals on that score are well known —in Vienna, in Geneva and in Stockholm. They remain in effect and retain their timeliness and importance in full.

Europe should be mentioned separately. The task of preventing the level of military confrontation in Europe from growing any further is more urgent than ever before. The European home is a common home where geography and history have strongly bonded together the destiny of many countries and peoples.

It is only by a collective effort, by following the reasonable norms of international contacts and cooperation, that Europeans can preserve their home, can make it better and safer.

We proceed from the view that Europe, which gave the world so much in the sphere of culture, science, technology, and advanced social thought, is also capable of setting an example in the solution of the most complex problems of present-day international life. The basis for this was laid down in Helsinki ten years ago. It is our profound conviction that the whole world, including the United States, stands ultimately to gain from the positive developments in Europe. We have been and shall be working for the sake of the principles and policy of détente which is being consolidated more vigorously on the long-suffering European continent and for the overcoming of the roadblocks of the past and the consequences of the confrontation of recent years.

I would like to make a special mention here of trade and economic relations. The business circles of many Western countries would like to establish wider economic contacts with us. I heard this mentioned by very influential representatives of those circles. They were talking about readiness to conclude large contracts and to start vast joint projects. Those politicians who try to impose restrictions on this natural striving for businesslike cooperation in the hope of "punishing" someone, of inflicting damage on a partner, are simply acting, to my mind, unwisely.

The fallacy of this policy has long become obvious. It would be much more useful to exert efforts for a different purpose, for ensuring that trade, scientific and technical exchanges consolidate the material basis of confidence and accord.

We will continue to cooperate closely with our Warsaw Treaty allies and with all the other countries of the socialist community in the struggle for lasting peace and cooperation among nations in Europe and on other continents. The states participating in the Warsaw Treaty Organization will under no circumstances foresake the security of their peoples. They will pool their efforts to an ever-growing extent within the CMEA framework to accelerate scientific and technical progress and socioeconomic development.

Interaction with the nonaligned movement, including comprehensive cooperation with the Republic of India, whose people and leaders we hold in profound respect, has a great role to play in the improvement of international relations.

The Soviet leadership attaches serious importance to the Asian and Pacific region. The Soviet Union's longest borders are in Asia. There we have loyal friends and reliable allies, from neighboring Mongolia to socialist Vietnam. It is extremely important to ensure that this region is not a source of tension and an area of armed confrontation. We stand for the broadening of political dialogue among all the states in the region in the interests of peace, good-neighborliness, mutual trust and cooperation.

We welcome the stand of the People's Republic of China, which is opposed to the militarization of space, and its statement renouncing the first use of nuclear weapons.

We stand for better relations with Japan and it is our conviction that this is possible. It stems even from the mere fact that our countries are next-door neighbors. Also, the interests of the USSR and Japan cannot help coinciding in the vital matter of removing the nuclear threat.

We have established relations of equal cooperation with many states of Latin America, Africa and the Middle East. The Soviet Union will continue to work purposefully to develop these relations. We value especially our close contacts with socialist-oriented countries on different continents.

The peoples of the whole world are today facing a host of questions which can only be resolved jointly and only under conditions of peace. A few dozen years ago serious ecological problems were virtually nonexistent. But already our generation is witnessing the mass extermination of forests, extinction of animals, contamination of rivers and other water bodies, and growing desertification. What will the world be like that future generations will see? Will they be able to live in it if the voracious destruction of nature is not stopped and if the economic, technical and scientific achievements of our time are not directed to meet the needs of ensuring conditions for the existence and progress of man and his environment but at perfecting weapons of destruction?

Or take energy. We are now living for the most part at the expense of the Earth's depths. But what was lying virtually on the surface is being exhausted, and the further development of these resources is growing more and more expensive and becoming more and more arduous. Moreover, this source is not eternal.

Dangerous upheavals can be caused by the growing gap between a handful of highly industrialized capitalist nations and those developing countries—and there is an overwhelming majority of them—whose lot is poverty, hunger and lack of hope. The gap between these two poles in the world is becoming ever wider, and relations between them ever more antagonistic. It cannot be otherwise unless the industrialized capitalist nations alter their self-serving policies.

Mankind is capable of resolving all these problems today if it pools its forces and intellect. Then it will be possible to scale new heights in the development of our civilization.

Militarism is an enemy of nations. The arms race, which whipped up the thirst for gain of the military-industrial complex, is sheer madness. It affects the vital interests of all countries and peoples. This is why, when instead of the elimination of nuclear weapons the project of the arms race into space is proposed to us as well, we respond with a firm "no." We say "no" because such a step means a new round in the mad squandering of funds. We say "no" because this means the heightening of the threat already looming darkly over the world. We say "no" because life itself calls not for a competition in armaments, but for joint action for the good of peace.

The Soviet Union is a decisive advocate of the development of international life in this direction.

On the initiative of the USSR work involving scientists from different countries has begun on the Tokomak thermonuclear reactor project, which opens up an opportunity to resolve the energy problem radically. According to scientists, it is possible to create as early as within this century a "terrestrial sun"—an inexhaustible source of thermonuclear energy. We note with satisfaction that it was agreed in Geneva to carry on with that important project.

It is our country that submitted to the United Nations an extensive and detailed program of peaceful cooperation in space, and for the development of a universal space organization to coordinate the efforts of countries in the exploration and development of space. There are truly boundless possibilities for such cooperation. They include fundamental research projects and the application of their findings in geology, medicine, materials studies and studies of the climate and the environment. They include the development of global satellite-aided communication systems and remote probing of the Earth. They, finally, include the development of new space technology, such as large orbital scientific stations and various manned spacecraft, their use in the interests of all the peoples, and the eventual industrialization of near-Earth space. All this constitutes a realistic alternative to the "Star Wars" plans. It is oriented toward a peaceful future for all humankind.

The Soviet Union was one of the active participants in the conclusion of an international convention to regulate the economic utilization of the resources of the world's oceans. The accomplishment of this task is also vastly important for ensuring the progress of human civilization and in broadening and multiplying the possibilities open to present-day society.

We offer the whole world, including the world of capitalist

states, a broad, long-term and comprehensive program of mutually beneficial cooperation, a program incorporating new opportunities which are being opened before mankind by the age of scientific and technical revolution. Cooperation between two such states as the Soviet Union and the United States could play a far from minimal role in carrying out this program.

Our policy is clearly a policy of peace and cooperation.

Comrades, the successes of our foreign policy are inherent in the nature of the socialist system. The Communist Party senses well and appreciates highly the nationwide support for its domestic and foreign policy. This support is manifested in the daily practical work of millions upon millions of people. The results achieved in the national economy mean not only an economic, but also an important moral and political result attesting to the rightness of our course.

We face important undertakings which are not easy. "However, difficulty does not imply impossibility," the great Lenin taught us. "The important thing is to be confident that the path chosen is the right one, this confidence multiplying a hundredfold revolutionary energy and revolutionary enthusiasm...." The Party and the Soviet people have this confidence, which multiplies our strength.

We are confident that every Communist, every worker, every farmer, every engineer and scientist, every work collective, will be aware of high responsibility to the Motherland, will perform their duty.

We are confident that everything will be done at every work place to ensure that the plans of 1986 are successfully fulfilled and overfulfilled, that our country becomes still richer and mightier, and that the cause of peace on Earth is strengthened and victorious.

November 27, 1985

6

A MESSAGE
TO THE PERUGIA-ASSISI
PEACE MARCHERS

Y HEARTFELT greetings to the Perugia-Assisi peace marchers.

The Soviet people hold close to their hearts your desire to achieve progress in safeguarding peace and stopping the dangerous development of events in the international arena.

The Damoclean sword of nuclear catastrophe and "Star Wars" has now been raised over humanity. But we have faith that through the common, concerted actions of all nations and all peace-loving forces, it is still possible to ward off this threat and start a real reduction in armaments.

It is with these aims in mind that the Soviet Union proposed the comprehensive program of constructive measures for an improvement in the international situation and an end to the arms race.

The Soviet Union has just proposed to the U.S. Government that we come to terms concerning a full ban on space strike weapons for both sides and a drastic reduction, by fifty per cent, of nuclear weapons capable of reaching each other's territory. We have shown our good will convincingly and palpably. It is now the turn of our negotiating partners.

As for your very urgent slogan concerning freezing military expenditures, I shall recall that back in 1984 the Soviet Union and other Warsaw Treaty member-states suggested to the NATO countries that the two sides start talks on a mutual freeze in military expenditure and its subsequent reduction.

The anti-war movement has an important question to put in resolving the destiny of humanity: Should there be peace or a war of annihilation? Political and ideological differences recede when life on Earth is put at stake.

Your march and other actions by peace campaigners are a sizable contribution to the lofty struggle against the launching of the arms race to the heights of space, for a peaceful life for all nations.

I wish you and the entire anti-war movement in Italy great success.

7

A MESSAGE TO THE SPECIAL JUBILEE SESSION OF THE U.N. GENERAL ASSEMBLY

I greet the esteemed representatives of the member states of the United Nations Organization, who have gathered in New York for a special jubilee session of the UN General Assembly on the occasion of the twenty-fifth anniversary of the adoption of the Declaration on the Granting of Independence to the Colonial Countries and Peoples.

The Soviet people are most deeply gratified by the fact that this Declaration, which became an international anti-colonial manifesto, was adopted at the Fifteenth Session of the UN General Assembly in 1960 on the USSR's initiative.

The Declaration, drawn up by the collective efforts of many states, has contributed to consolidating the freedom-loving forces of all continents, mobilizing them for resolute actions with the aim of doing away with the disgraceful system of colonialism and ensuring the right of the peoples to self-determination and independence, the right to build their future freely, without outside interference.

Over a short historical period, colonial empires have collapsed, tens of new independent states of Asia, Africa, Latin America and Oceania have become full-fledged members of the United Nations. The growing role of these states in the international arena is today's reality.

Yet the aims set forth in the Declaration have not been fully achieved so far. The United Nations cannot reconcile itself to the fact that the peoples of nearly twenty colonial and dependent territories are still deprived of the legitimate right to freedom and independence. Wishing to preserve their domination, the imperialist powers impose on these territories various forms of neo-colonial status and turn them into their military-strategic strongpoints and bridgeheads for aggression. The annexationist actions with regard to the trust territory of the Pacific Islands are a striking example of this.

In southern Africa, the racist regime of Pretoria, backed by its Western patrons, is trying to perpetuate a colonialist-racist system. Flouting the decisions of the United Nations and the demands of the world public, the racists of South Africa are pursuing a criminal apartheid policy, opposing the granting of independence to the people of Namibia and launching acts of aggression against neighboring African countries.

The policy of colonialism in any form and manifestation, including racism and apartheid, is incompatible with the UN Charter and the Declaration on decolonization. The conscience of all honest people of the world cannot reconcile itself to the preservation of the seats of colonialism on our planet.

It is the duty of the United Nations to take urgent measures to implement the Declaration in full, so that all colonial peoples and trust territories should gain genuine political and economic independence and take a worthy place in the international community of states.

It is the duty of the United Nations to contribute in every way to accelerating the process of decolonization in the economic field and restructuring international economic relations on a fair and democratic basis. The United Nations should raise its voice against the exploitation of the developing countries by transnationals. It should oppose plunder of their natural resources and their being stifled by debts. It should support their actions against "cultural", "informational" and other forms of neocolonialism.

Implementation of these important tasks depends, to a decisive extent, on progress in strengthening universal peace and international security and on ending the ruinous arms race and returning to a policy of relaxation of international tension.

The Soviet Union will continue to make every effort in the struggle for full and consistent implementation of the Declaration on the Granting of Independence to the Colonial Countries and Peoples and actively contribute to UN activities in the matter of the final elimination of colonialism, racism and apartheid.

Mikhail Gorbachev
October 17, 1985

8

A MESSAGE
TO THE
U.N. SECRETARY GENERAL
AND PARTICIPANTS IN THE
U.N. GENERAL ASSEMBLY
COMMEMORATIVE SESSION

ESTEEMED Mr. Secretary General,

I greet you and all those who attend the UN General Assembly's anniversary session to mark forty years of the United Nations Organization.

The United Nations owes its birth to the victory over fascism and militarism won by the freedom-loving peoples. It is only natural that the UN Charter proclaims in its very first lines the United Nations' determination to save succeeding generations from the scourge of war, to practice tolerance and live in peace with one another as good neighbors.

The UN Charter, which became valid on October 24, 1945, the date recognized as the inauguration of the UN, has stood the test of time. The Organization has become an important factor in the system of international relations. The United Nations also has contributed to helping humanity avoid another world war for the past forty years.

Today, however, it is more essential than ever before to say that the principal task set by the UN Charter has not yet been accomplished. The guarantees for a durable peace have not been created. Today the joint efforts of states and peoples are needed more than ever to deliver humanity from the threat of a nuclear catastrophe.

What is needed above all for this purpose in practical terms is to put an end to the arms race on Earth and keep it out of space.

What is also required are fresh efforts to calm regional sites of tension and to remove the last vestiges of colonialism in all its manifestations.

The United Nations has many other pressing tasks: To facilitate, through real disarmament measures, the release of resources for the purposes of development, and the overcoming of backwardness, hunger, disease and poverty. The reshaping of international economic relations on a just and democratic basis and ensuring genuine human rights and liberties, most notably the right to a peaceful life, should also serve these purposes.

We speak about all this because we are firmly convinced that because the Organization's fortieth anniversary is such an important event, the prime attention of its member states should be directed at making UN activities still more effective and fruitful.

The Soviet Union, one of the founders of the United Nations and a permanent member of its Security Council, will make every effort, as always, to facilitate the world organization's successful fulfillment of its lofty mission in strict compliance with its Charter.

Mikhail Gorbachev
October 25, 1985

9

A REPLY
TO AN APPEAL
FROM THE LEADERS
OF THE CLUB OF ROME

ESTEEMED Dr. King and
Professor Pestel,
I am very grateful for your appeal which I have thoroughly studied.

I fully agree with you that the problems of war and peace hold, undoubtedly, the uppermost place among present-day international problems since they have a direct bearing on the preservation of civilization and life on Earth. It must be clear to all that the arms race, which is picking up at ever faster rates and acquiring new qualitative parameters, constitutes the main danger to the future of the whole world.

The Soviet Union is persistently seeking ways to end the arms race so as to embark on disarmament, and proposes to achieve agreement on the whole range of questions related to preventing the militarization of space and terminating the arms race on Earth. Precisely such an aim is pursued by a comprehensive program of constructive measures advanced recently by the Soviet Union, measures aimed at cardinal improvement of the international situation. In the framework of that program we proposed to the Government of the USA to come to terms on the total prohibition of space strike arms for both sides and to reduce really radically, by fifty per cent, the nuclear arms capable of reaching each other's territory. As you know, these are far

---

The Club of Rome is one of the influential international organizations that actively supports the termination of the arms race, an end to confrontation and a return to détente. The club's President, Alexander King, and member of the club's Executive Committee, E. Pestel, recently sent a letter to the General Secretary of the CPSU Central Committee Mikhail Gorbachev. The letter says that the problem of war and peace undoubtedly holds the uppermost place in the range of contemporary problems related to preserving humanity and civilization as it exists today.

The authors of the letter point out that international trade in arms represents one of the sources of the arms race, and urge the United States and the USSR to set an example in ending that trade, specifically arms deliveries to developing countries. The whole world would assess this as a remarkable act attesting to wise statesmanship by the heads of the two powers, the authors of the letter concluded.

from the only proposals of ours.

We approach the question of international trade in conventional armaments you posed in the context of our line of curtailing the arms race.

In this connection I would like to recall that the talks between the USSR and the USA on the limitation of sales and deliveries of conventional armaments started back in 1977. Work has been carried out toward coming to terms on the political, legal, military and technical criteria of permissibility or impermissibility of the sales and deliveries of armaments, as well as the aspects connected with involving other suppliers and studying the possibility of introducing additional restrictions for separate regions.

However, sharp changes toward increasing the weight of the "regional approach" were made in the U.S. position at the December 1978 round, that is, when possible approaches to settling the matter started taking shape. In accordance with the "regional approach," the Americans demanded that those regions which account for the bulk of the U.S. arms supplies be excluded from the discussion. The United States disrupted the talks unilaterally.

No changes took place in the U.S. stand either in the course of the meeting of the heads of the delegations at these talks or at the meeting held in September 1979 in accordance with the Vienna Communiqué on meetings between the General Secretary of the Central Committee of the Communist Party of the Soviet Union and the President of the United States of June 15, 1979.

It is not the Soviet Union that is to blame for the lack of progress in settling the matter. The Political Declaration of the Warsaw Treaty Member States adopted in Prague on January 5, 1983 emphasizes the expediency of the resumption of the Talks on the Limitation of Sales and Deliveries of Conventional Armaments.

It is the United States that refuses to resume such talks with the USSR. The directive of the President of the United States of July 8, 1981 says clearly that the United States views conventional arms supply as an important element of its global system of defense and an indispensable component of its foreign policy.

We share your opinion that the sales and deliveries of conventional armaments are a dangerous channel for the spread of the arms race to different areas of the world, and are conducive to the emergence of seats of tension and conflicts there.

Thus, it is clear that it is not the USSR that is responsible for the impasse in this important matter.

The Soviet Union stands for the limitation of international sales and deliveries of conventional armaments, for the resumption of appropriate Soviet-American talks and progress at them. The Soviet Union does not object to drawing other states into the consideration of this topical matter.

In conclusion I would like to wish the Club of Rome successes in its useful work for the advancement of the ideas of peace and in the noble activity for purposes of ending the arms race and achieving disarmament.

Yours respectfully,
Mikhail Gorbachev
October 25, 1985

10

A REPLY TO
THE JOINT MESSAGE
OF THE LEADERS
OF SIX STATES

To Mr. Raul Alfonsin, President of Argentina,
  Mr. Miguel de la Madrid, President of Mexico,
  Mr. Olof Palme, Prime Minister of Sweden,
  Mr. Rajiv Gandhi, Prime Minister of India,
  Mr. Julius Nyerere, President of Tanzania
  Mr. Andreas Papandreou, Prime Minister of Greece

DEAR Sirs,

Your joint message has been studied most attentively by the Soviet leaders. It confirms that we have common goals, that your proposals as to the cessation of the arms race, particularly the nuclear arms race, and the prevention of the militarization of space are consonant with our approach.

You have hopes, and with good reason, for the coming Soviet-American summit in Geneva and expect it to bring positive changes in international relations. For our part, we actively urge the conclusion at the meeting of concrete, tangible agreements that would promote the strengthening of security and trust in the world, and open up the possibility of halting the accelerating process of stockpiling and modernization of weapons. This is what the peoples of the world are waiting for.

Understanding its responsibility for the fate of the world, the Soviet Union has advanced a set of new initiatives covering practically all aspects of ending the arms race and promoting disarmament. We have stated that we are prepared to agree to reduce by half Soviet and American nuclear arms capable of reaching each other's territory if the development of space strike arms is banned. This is a real practical formula for preventing an arms race in space and for making truly drastic reductions in nuclear arms on Earth. The USSR has also taken, recently in particular, a number of unilateral steps in these directions, which are well known.

I would like to touch upon a matter which you particularly emphasize in your message, namely, that of the declaration of a twelve-month moratorium on nuclear explosions on the part of the USSR and the USA.

We share your assessment of the significance of such a measure. You have every grounds for linking the cessation of tests with hopes for erecting a sturdy barrier to the nuclear arms race, with a turn toward effectively eliminating nuclear weapons.

Indeed, the cessation of nuclear tests would make it possible to sharply decelerate, and in many respects actually preclude, the upgrading of nuclear weapons, development of new types thereof, and the intensification of their already lethal effect. In such conditions the nuclear arms race would be significantly undermined.

This is why the Soviet Union attaches so much importance to and works perseveringly and consistently for a complete and universal ban on nuclear weapon tests.

On August 6, attempting to break the deadlock in solving this problem, the USSR unilaterally banned all nuclear explosions till the end of the year. At the same time, we stated that the moratorium would stay in effect longer if the United States, on its part, joined it, likewise refraining from conducting nuclear explosions. So, whether the Soviet moratorium will remain in effect beyond the set date depends entirely on the United States.

There now exists a real possibility of taking a decisive and historic (in the full sense of this word) step to halt tests once and for all. As for the Soviet Union, I repeat that we can extend our moratorium beyond January 1, 1986 if the United States joins it. Moreover, we are prepared now, today, for an indefinite treaty ban on all nuclear weapon tests.

If political will were displayed, it would be quite possible, we believe, to solve the problem of verification. The present state of national technical means in the possession of the USSR and the United States allows both sides to determine easily whether nuclear tests are being conducted or not. The latest facts confirm this.

In addition, in reaching an accord on a complete and universal ban on nuclear weapon tests, other mutually acceptable verification methods, including those involving the use of the possibilities mentioned in your message, could be sought.

In order to solve the question of a universal ban on nuclear weapon tests, as well as that of a temporary moratorium on nuclear weapon tests, each side must be willing to make compromises, taking into account the security interests of the other. Any hopes of achieving unilateral advantages in this sphere are groundless.

We continue to believe in the strength of good example, in the triumph of common sense, which should take the upper hand in the long run when the point at issue is the very existence of civilization.

I would like to express hope that the efforts in this direction, stimulated by the opinion of the influential leaders of the states signatories to the Delhi Declaration which represent different continents on our planet, will bear fruit. You can always depend on the Soviet Union in this noble endeavor.

Mikhail Gorbachev
November 8, 1985

11

A SPEECH
BEFORE NOBEL PEACE
PRIZE WINNERS

Iᴛ ɪs with pleasure that I accept an address signed by outstanding scientists who are Nobel Prize winners. I would like to say right away that the Soviet leadership views this address as a document of tremendous significance to all humankind. The appeal it makes for the two great powers to secure a turn for the better in international affairs, put an end to the arms race and prevent the militarization of outer space is fully consonant with the sentiments in our country and the practical intentions of its leadership.

Our time is, without exaggeration, a crucial moment in history. Humankind has now reached a point which calls for particular wisdom in decision-making, care in considering moves, discretion in action and regard not only for our own country's national interests but also for the interests of the entire world community. I think it is the realization of this fact that also underlies the initiative made by the Nobel Prize winners.

In the USSR we believe that there is no task more important and pressing today than to close the channels for the continued stockpiling of nuclear arms, the increasingly sophisticated kinds of these weapons, while shutting the door securely on armaments in outer space. This is consistent with the views and proposals we are taking to the Soviet-American meeting in a few days.

Our approach to this meeting is open and fair. We go to Geneva completely aware of the responsibility resting on the leaders of all countries but, primarily, of the USSR and the United States. We go there for serious and productive work and, I should say, with our hands not empty.

The Soviet Union stands for the meeting to help in actually resolving the key issues of our times, those of enhancing international peace and security, improving relations between the USSR and the United States, checking the arms race and preventing its extension to outer space.

We are deeply convinced that it is especially important

today that every thinking person be fully aware of one's personal responsibility for warding off the war threat. And it is only natural for scientists, who perhaps have a clearer idea than others of the likely aftermath of a nuclear war, to raise their voice against wars, be they terrestrial wars or "star" wars. This is also how I interpret the message conveyed by you. Our country highly values the humanist tradition of true scientists who have always taken an active stand on the issue of war and peace, a tradition initiated by Niels Bohr, Albert Einstein and Frederic Joliot-Curie.

Our time is truly the "gold age" of science. The bounds of knowledge are extending exceptionally fast. All the way from the microcosm to outer space, human reason is penetrating such depths and secrets of nature as seemed out of reach only a short time ago. Making full use of the results of this cognition would make it possible to enrich man's material and intellectual life in terms of quality.

And isn't it a terrible paradox of the twentieth century that achievements in science directed to developing weapons of mass annihilation threaten the very existence of the human race?

The issues of war and peace have been put in the foreground by the objective course of development itself.

Scientists' influential say and competent opinion can, and are called upon, to play a big role in awakening the people to reality and urging them on to vigorous action to stop and reverse the arms race and start reducing armaments.

You are right in stressing in your message that courage today is required not in preparing for war but in achieving peace. This is even more true since the arms race has reached a critical point. Even today advances in military technology have made arms control extremely difficult. We have come right down to a line beyond which the situation may become altogether uncontrollable.

Whether strike weapons will make it to outer space or be barred from it is an all-important question. The answer to it is decisive in the course of developments in the world for many years ahead. Can there be any peaceful future and strategic stability if yet another mortal danger, one from space, emerges in addition to the missiles already in silos and under the ocean?

Imagine what the world will be in this case in ten or twenty years. Waves of all manner of strike weapons will be rushing overhead everywhere, from the edge of the atmosphere at an altitude of a hundred kilometers to geostationary orbits, above all people inhabiting our planet.

The Soviet people, who have lived for forty years surrounded by American "forward-based" weaponry, strongly reject the very possibility of its spread to outer space and the very prospect of having it overhead, above their homes.

And how will ordinary Americans, who have not yet gotten accustomed to having others' weapons on their borders, either on Earth or in space, feel in this case? I think that tension in relations between our countries will escalate to a point unprecedented even by today's standards and will be even more difficult to control.

The militarization of outer space will put a heavy psychological burden on people in all countries and bring about an atmosphere of universal instability and uncertainty.

The question arises: What's the purpose of all this? By the way, it is appropriate to ask this question as well: Doesn't the very fact of deployment of weapons by one state in outer space, above the territory of other states, constitute a breach of their sovereignty?

Soviet people in their letters often ask what the Soviet Union will do if the United States, in spite of everything, embarks on the development, testing and deployment of a multi-tier antimissile defense. We have already said that the USSR will find an effective answer which, in our opinion, will meet the demand of maintaining strategic equilibrium and its stability. But if this happens, the case in point will be a new round of the arms race.

As is known, there were no weapons in outer space until now. If they appear there it will be an exceptionally difficult undertaking to bring them back from space. And it is totally unsubstantiated to expect that the development of space strike weapons will lead to the disappearance of nuclear weapons on Earth. The history of the development of new types of weapons and the existing realities are convincing testimony to the contrary.

Does the logic that it is necessary to arm oneself to the teeth in order to disarm make sense at all? In other words: Why should one develop missiles to destroy missiles when there is a different, more dependable and safer way and, what is most important, a way leading directly to the goal. This is to reach accords on the reduction and subsequent complete elimination of the existing missiles.

It is clear from all points of view and from the position of common sense as well that the second way is the only reasonable one. We are for it.

You know that our country is prepared to see halved the number of warheads capable of reaching the territory of the United States and the USSR. We have stopped all tests of nuclear weapons. We have unilaterally reduced medium-range missiles in Europe as well. We are ready to sign a treaty of nonaggression, to agree to the establishment of zones free from nuclear and chemical weapons.

All these steps of ours, just like many proposals that are now on the negotiating table, taken together and individually provide an opportunity to improve the international situation substantially, to lessen the threat of nuclear conflict and to pave the way toward complete nuclear disarmament. We realize perfectly well that to live with the perpetual threat of nuclear weapons is a dismal prospect for humankind.

What alternative to that does the Strategic Defense Initiative provide? In our firmly held view, only an unlimited and mutually accelerating race in so-called "defensive" and "offensive" arms.

I have more than once had to characterize the SDI politically. I won't stress yet another time its clearly imperial tilt toward trying to ensure superiority—both military and technological—over other states.

I will dwell on another aspect. It is said that the SDI will ensure a breakthrough in the field of technology. But even if we assume that its realization will promote scientific and technological progress, the question still remains: At what price will this be achieved? It is absolutely clear that the price will be the development of new suicidal arms systems. More and more people, in the U.S. also, are coming to understand this.

We are in favor of an essentially different way of speeding up the progress in science and technology. We are for competition in technology and constructive cooperation in the conditions of a durable and just peace.

Isn't outer space itself a highly promising arena of international cooperation? We have just now started exploring it in the interests of science and man's practical activity. But how much has been achieved within a short period of time! The first sputnik, the first man in space, the first man on the Moon, the landings on Venus and Mars, an excellent map of Venus.

These are just initial steps. And it is necessary to make the exploration of boundless expanses of outer space a joint undertaking of states.

We have submitted for the United Nations' consideration an extensive program of peaceful cooperation in space. The USSR proposes to create a world space organization, which would be the center for coordinating the efforts of all countries in this enterprise.

This means fundamental scientific research and the launching of interplanetary ships, for instance to Mars, for these purposes.

This means the application of the results of space research in the spheres of biology, medicine, materials science, weather forecasting, studies of the climate and nature, for the creation of a global satellite communication system and remote sensing of the Earth's surface and making studies of the world ocean.

This, finally, means creation by joint efforts and use in the interests of all peoples of new space equipment, including large orbital scientific stations, various manned ships and, in the future, the industrialization of near-Earth space.

Naturally, we are prepared for peaceful cooperation in

space on a bilateral basis, too, with those states that show interest in it. This fully applies to the United States as well.

You remember the Soyuz-Apollo linkup in 1975 which fascinated humankind. Something is being done now, too: We are conducting studies of Venus and Halley's Comet jointly with American scientists in the framework of the international project called "Vega." We take part in the search and rescue program from space jointly with other countries.

This, however, is just a small fraction of what could be done jointly. It is unreasonable to let such opportunities slip by.

By all indications, much interest is being shown among the American public, scientists and in the U.S. Congress in the resumption of cooperation, and specific projects are being advanced. We are prepared to consider serious proposals of this kind.

Both military programs and peaceful projects in space, including research, are costly undertakings. So, the greater the reasons to choose the alternative of peaceful cooperation.

The mastering of thermonuclear synthesis is a promising area of international cooperation. This will provide humankind with a virtually unlimited source of energy, a sort of man-made Sun.

As is known, the idea of a controlled thermonuclear reaction was first advanced by Academician Igor Kurchatov in his well-known lecture in Great Britain back in 1956, when he familiarized scientists of many countries with the work of Soviet scientists.

The Tokamak international pilot thermonuclear reactor project has been under way in Vienna since 1978 on the initiative of the Soviet Union, with the participation of scientists from a number of Western European countries as well as from the United States and Japan.

Already it can be said that such a reactor is technically feasible, and specialists believe it can be built in the relatively near future, in any case, before the year 2000.

During the recent visit to Paris we expressed the appropriate considerations to French President François Mitterrand. He received our proposal positively. We deem it important, moreover, necessary, to pool the efforts of all states concerned in the implementation of thermonuclear synthesis, which will make it possible to solve one of the most acute global problems, the energy problem.

There are a lot of pressing tasks in the world today that require coordination and cooperation. I would like to emphasize again that the Soviet Union is firmly and consistently in favor of the broadest cooperation, of pooling the efforts of states in using the achievements of scientific and technical progress exclusively for peaceful purposes and humankind's progress. I can assure you that the Soviet Union does not lack the readiness or goodwill for this cooperation.

I wish you success in your fruitful scientific activity, in the noble field of upholding the cause of a world without arms, a world without wars.

November 13, 1985

A SPEECH
TO HONOR
THE PARTICIPANTS
IN THE NINTH ANNUAL
MEETING OF ASTEC

LADIES and gentlemen, comrades,

I am pleased to welcome in the Kremlin the participants in the annual meeting of the U.S.-USSR Trade and Economic Council (ASTEC). We value the extensive activities in which the Council has been engaged for ten years now in promoting contacts between American companies and Soviet foreign trade organizations. We value that fact particularly since, as you know, those were not easy years.

I also would like to address words of welcome to United States Secretary of Commerce, Mr. Baldridge. We appreciate his presence here.

The current meeting provides more confirmation that it is quite possible—and today, I would say, indispensable—to develop cooperation among people, nations and states having different social systems and different ideologies.

Whether we like each other or not, we will have to live on this planet together. Hence our most important task—of which I spoke both in Geneva and afterwards—is to master the art of getting along together. And since this situation will be around for quite a while, we have to learn to live side by side in a civilized manner, as befits human beings.

This brings me to the question of commercial and economic as well as scientific and technological ties between the Soviet Union and the United States, or, put in more general terms, between East and West. We view those ties above all from a political standpoint. First, this is because politics is the field where we tackle the main question of our relationship, namely, the question of war and peace. All other aspects of our relations, including trade and economic ties, should serve this overriding objective. Second, this is because our two countries are economic giants fully able to live and develop without any trade with each other whatsoever.

This, in effect, is the way things are right now. Look at the facts. In our trade exchanges the United States, the largest trading power in the world, ranks thirteenth, lagging far behind Finland, Belgium and Austria. We ourselves are in sixteenth place among the U.S.'s foreign trade partners. The volume of U.S. imports from the USSR is roughly equal to what your country imports from the Republic of the Ivory Coast.

I regard this as no economic tragedy at all. Both of us will survive without each other, particularly since there is no lack of trading partners in the world today.

But is it normal from a political standpoint? My answer is definitely and emphatically No! In our dangerous world we simply cannot afford to neglect—nor have we the right to do so—the stabilizing factors in relations concerning trade and economic, scientific and technological ties. If we are to have a genuinely stable and enduring relationship capable of ensuring a lasting peace, it should be based, among other things, on well-developed business relations.

In this day and age each country and nation—the smallest as well as the biggest ones—regard independence as their highest value and spare no effort to defend it. Any yet we are witnessing the growing interdependence of states. This is a natural consequence of the development of the world economy today and at the same time an important factor for international stability. Such interdependence is to be welcomed. It can become a powerful incentive in building stable, normal and, I would even venture to say, friendly relations.

Dear guests,

We are fully conscious of the complexity of the tasks facing all of us. I know that there are among you senior executives of companies that are prominent in American military business. Let me say frankly: We believe that the military business exerts a dangerous influence on politics. In fact, we are not alone in thinking so. The very concept of the military-industrial complex was not formulated by Marxists but by a conservative Republican, President Dwight D. Eisenhower of the United States, who warned the American people of the negative role that can be played by that complex.

I am not saying this to reproach those of our guests who have contracts with the Pentagon. They have come to Moscow, and we welcome that fact, which, as I see it, testifies to the common sense of some representatives of military business. It would appear to me that some of them, as well as the U.S. business community as a whole, cannot remain indifferent to the economic and financial consequences for the country of excessive military expenditures as well as the consequences of a one-sided development of the economy caused by militarization.

As to the Soviet leadership, we are deeply convinced that cessation of the arms race serves the genuine vital interests of not only the Soviet Union but also the United States—if, of course, we are to address the crux of the matter rather than be guided only by the benefits of the moment accruing from any particular contract.

Learning to live in peace—and this, I believe, is the preeminent interest common to both of us—means not only to refrain from making war. The difference between living in the genuine sense of that word and languishing in fear of a new increase in the danger of war is that the former implies the development of varied contacts and cooperation, including trade.

Another reason why I believe that the development of trade and economic ties between our two countries is a political problem is that the main obstacles in their way are political rather than economic.

The first such obstacle is that the Soviet Union does not enjoy the so-called most-favored-nation treatment. The term itself may be misleading, the impression being that it implies a particularly favorable attitude on the part of the United States to those granted such treatment. However, American businessmen know full well that this is not so. In practice the MFN treatment is no more than the absence of discrimination, primarily in customs tariffs. I have been told that about 120 countries enjoy the MFN treatment in the United States.

The Soviet Union is being denied that treatment. And this, of course, creates obstacles in the way of our exporting many kinds of products to the United States, making it impossible for us to earn the money needed to purchase American products. After all, we cannot endlessly earn foreign currency, let us say, in Western Europe while spending it in the United States, for our trade partners will simply not appreciate that.

The second problem is the obstacles we have to face in the United States regarding credits. I don't have to prove to you experienced businessmen that there can be no serious trade without credits.

The third obstacle is the so-called "export controls," i.e. bans on the export of numerous products under the pretext that they can help in Soviet military production and thus prejudice U.S. security. There is a wealth of speculation on that score.

I would like first of all to say this: The allegation that the Soviet Union's defense potential is based almost entirely on purchased Western technology and that it cannot develop without it is complete nonsense. Those who have come up with that allegation simply forget what kind of country they are dealing with; they forget—or want to make others forget—that the Soviet Union is a country of advanced science and technology, a country of outstanding scientists and engineers and highly skilled workers.

Admittedly, like any other country, we rely—in military as well as civilian industries—on both our own and international scientific and technological achievements and international production know-how. That's life; it is inevitable, as demonstrated by the example of the United States itself. It is no secret, for instance, that a leading role in the development of nuclear weapons and missiles was played not by American science and scientists but by European, including Russian and Soviet, scientists.

The real facts of today, as well as the lessons of history, should not be forgotten. To put things in true perspective, let me cite some of those facts here.

It is a fact that theoretical foundations of rocket technology were discovered and formulated by the outstanding Russian scientist Tsiolkovsky, that the basic theory of multistage rockets originated in our country and that the first experimental rockets, and, finally, the first artificial Earth satellite were launched by our country, too, to say nothing of the first manned space flight.

One can speak at great length about the contributions made by Russian and Soviet scientists—from Mendeleyev to our time—to the development of modern chemistry. Let me just mention the fact that of the transuranic elements identified since 1950, a half were discovered by Soviet researchers.

The major, and in many respects decisive, contribution of Soviet scientists to the development of the chain reaction theory, the light and radiowaves theory and the discovery of lasers is also beyond dispute. Modern aerodynamics, very low-temperature and very high-pressure technologies and almost all the technologies used in modern metallurgy would be inconceivable without what has been done by Soviet scientists.

For all that, we are not saying that American corporations operate on technologies stolen from the Soviet Union.

Just like you, we are interested in the development of scientific and technological ties and cooperation, which is quite normal and legitimate. I want all of you in the United States to understand that the Soviet Union will not become a market for obsolete products, that we are going to buy only those items that meet high world standards. If the United States persists in its current policy, we will produce what we need on our own or buy it elsewhere.

Another obstacle to the development of our trade and economic ties is the policy of boycotts, embargoes, sanctions and broken trade contracts that has become a habit with the United States. You know what the results are: No particular harm has been done to the Soviet Union, while the commercial reputation of U.S. business and therefore its competitive position in the Soviet market have been seriously damaged. Our economic managers have lost confidence in the U.S. partners and therefore increasingly prefer other partners.

This is what happened with large contracts for the delivery of pipe-laying equipment and equipment for the Novolipetsk Iron and Steel Integrated Works and an aluminum plant in Siberia, to say nothing of oil- and gas-drilling and prospecting equipment, where the U.S. share in our purchases has currently fallen to less than half a percentage point. And, being better informed than I am of the existing situation in the world markets, you are aware of the fact that competition there is bound to become ever more intensive in the foreseeable future.

I will be absolutely frank with you: So long as those obstacles exist, there will be no normal development of Soviet-U.S. trade and other economic ties on a large scale. This is regrettable, but we are not going to beg the United States for anything.

However, should those political obstacles be removed, then I am sure broad prospects would open up before us. We are not competing with you in the world market or in the United States itself; in this respect you have more problems with your own allies than with us. But we can become partners—natural partners who, I can assure you, will be honest and reliable.

Naturally, this will require work on both sides, including better knowledge of each other's markets and an improved mechanism for economic cooperation. I am aware that we are not without fault here either. The Soviet Government takes a fairly critical view of our foreign trade organizations, too. We believe that new forms of production and scientific and technological cooperation can be found.

We are now engaged in a major effort in that regard with the socialist countries. We view greater economic integration with them as a most important task. We also intend to expand trade and other forms of economic cooperation with Western Europe, Japan and the developing countries.

We would not want our economic relations with the United States to be left out of that process—both for the political reasons that I have referred to and for economic reasons as well. We have great plans for our economic, scientific and technological development. And for that we would like to make the fullest possible use of the additional opportunities inherent in international cooperation, including those with the United States. One can contemplate major long-term projects and numerous medium-size and even small business deals which would be of interest both to giant corporations and to small and medium-size businesses. Provided that the situation is normalized and a sound political and contractual basis is established for the development of trade and economic relations, we shall have both things to buy from you and things to sell to you.

We might suggest that U.S. companies and businesses participate in our programs of further developing the energy sector of our economy. We could also consider the possibility of giving American businesses and companies a share in our major effort to radically modernize machine-tool building and other machine-building industries. Should American companies find it worthwhile, they might, perhaps, become involved in the work which is under way in our country in the agroindustrial complex, in chemistry and petrochemistry and in the production of sets of machines and equipment to introduce intensive technologies in land cultivation and animal husbandry.

All this, however, requires a display of political will. Economic relations have to be built on a long-term basis. Guarantees are needed that some political wind chill will not once again begin to freeze business ties.

And now let me go back to politics. This session of the U.S.-USSR Trade and Economic Council is taking place just three weeks after the Soviet-American meeting in Geneva. This fact makes the current session quite special. As I see it, its purpose is to analyze the potential for trade and economic cooperation between the Soviet Union and the United States and to see what should be done in the best interests of both the Soviet and American peoples.

The realization of the fact that the present state of Soviet-U.S. relations is unsatisfactory and dangerous was the main reason that brought President Reagan and myself to Geneva for our meeting and negotiations. I am sure that the President of the United States felt, as I did, that during those days the eyes of hundreds of millions of men and women, and even children, in our two countries and, in fact, in all other countries were focused on Geneva. And those eyes expressed both hope and anxiety.

I can tell you frankly that feeling all that was not an easy experience. However, neither myself nor, I believe, the President thought it possible to shirk that enormous burden of human concerns and aspirations.

Bearing in mind how difficult the road to Geneva was, it may be said that some success was achieved there. It is, however, only a first step. And every step that may follow will require still greater effort, a greater readiness to listen, a greater willingness and ability to understand and accommodate each other and, what is most important, a willingness to learn the most difficult art of reaching agreements on an equal and mutually acceptable basis, without which we will never be able to solve any serious problem.

In other words, we have entered a particularly crucial period, when words, intentions and political statements should be translated into concrete decisions and action. What I have in mind, as you understand, are decisions and actions that would contribute to putting Soviet-American relations on an even keel and to a general improvement in the world political climate.

Many U.S. businessmen are known for their well-developed enterprising spirit, a knack for innovation and an ability to identify untapped growth opportunities. I am convinced that today the best, genuinely promising possibilities of that kind are to be found not in pursuit of destruction and death but in the quest for peace and in a joint effort for the sake of equal and mutually beneficial cooperation among all countries and peoples. This is the essence of life, and the benefits to be derived from it are indisputable.

Allow me to wish the U.S.-USSR Trade and Economic Council success in its useful activities.

Thank you all for your attention.

December 10, 1985

13

A TALK WITH U.S. SECRETARY OF COMMERCE MALCOLM BALDRIDGE

DURING the conversation Mikhail Gorbachev pointed out the importance of the Geneva summit meeting, and above all the opportunities it provided for normalizing Soviet-American relations and improving the international situation in general. He stressed that although only the first steps had been taken and that the Soviet Union and the United States continued to be separated by major disagreements, especially on the fundamental issues of security, the overall result of the meeting was still positive.

The main point is that a discussion has started concerning the explosive and acute problems that have been piling up for years. It is high time to begin resolving these. The true significance of everything agreed upon in Geneva, of course, can manifest itself only in practical politics.

As far as the Soviet side is concerned, it treats the accords reached in Geneva most seriously and will seek improvement not only in the general atmosphere, but also in the content of Soviet-U.S. relations. It will do this on the basis of mutual respect and complete equality without any discrimination. In a spirit of fair interaction with the United States, the Soviet Union is prepared to work to reverse the arms race while keeping it out of space and to improving the world situation. We have the right to expect a similar approach also from the United States.

All this, Mikhail Gorbachev said, fully applies to the commercial and economic sphere as well. The Soviet Union treats most seriously the intention of both sides, recorded in the joint statement on the Geneva summit, to develop trade and economic relations. Regrettably, the situation existing in this field can by no means be called satisfactory. The reason is well known, namely the discriminatory policies of the United States and its attempts to use trade as an instrument of political pressure on the USSR.

It is clear, however, that this policy has outlived its usefulness.

The Soviet Union, Mikhail Gorbachev said, is a reliable and promising partner. The Soviet market's potentials are enormous, especially now that the Soviet Union is tackling the challenging task of accelerating its social and economic development. The trading partners of the Soviet Union in other countries know this well and are making use of these opportunities in no small way to their benefit.

Mikhail Gorbachev expressed satisfaction with the fact that the U.S. business community, as demonstrated, for instance, by the American-Soviet Trade and Economic Council's meeting, is showing interest in broadening mutually advantageous trade with the Soviet Union. In it they will find complete understanding on the part of the relevant Soviet organizations. There are substantial potentials for large-scale and long-term trade and economic relations between the Soviet Union and the United States. It is up to the American side to use them.

Malcolm Baldridge spoke generally about developing U.S.-Soviet trade, especially after the Geneva summit, and reiterated the American business community's interests. At the same time he pointed to the constraints, imposed by the U.S. Administration and Congress, that hinder the development of commercial relations with the USSR.

Also discussed during the conversation were some other aspects of Soviet-U.S. relations.

December 10, 1985

14

A MEETING WITH PRESIDENT OF THE FRENCH NATIONAL ASSEMBLY LOUIS MERMOZ

DURING A CONVERSATION held in a friendly and constructive atmosphere, the sides discussed a number of international problems and prospects for Soviet-French relations.

It was noted with satisfaction that relations between the USSR and France have received a fresh impetus following the Soviet-French summit meeting in Paris. The Soviet Union, Mikhail Gorbachev said, favors the broadest development of friendly ties with France.

Turning to the international situation, Mikhail Gorbachev said that the USSR did not see a more important and urgent task than curbing the arms race and using every opportunity to achieve a radical turn for the better in international affairs. New ways of thinking about foreign policy and new approaches to relations between states are needed today as never before in the past. At the recent Soviet-American summit meeting the Soviet Union was guided by exactly such an approach.

A frank and on the whole useful discussion was initiated in Geneva on the most burning questions of our time. The pivotal issue is the termination of the arms race on Earth and prevention of one in space. Some points of contact emerged between the positions of the USSR and the USA on this fundamental problem. However, the main obstacle to resolving it, the U.S. "Star Wars" program, remains. The implementation of this program can lead only to an uncontrollable arms race in every direction. The Soviet Union hopes that the American side has not yet spoken its final word on this matter. The role and responsibility of West European states in this context are exceptionally great too.

Mikhail Gorbachev stressed that the Soviet Union's readiness to do everything within its power to resolve disarmament problems has been demonstrated by practical steps. For instance, during the visit to France it was announced that the Soviet Union on its initiative had withdrawn from operational duty the SS-20 missiles deployed additionally in the European zone and that stationary facilities for those missiles would be dismantled within the next two months. The USSR has lived up to its promise. Dismantling operations have been completed.

The situation in Europe and the world today is not quite what it was a few months ago, Mikhail Gorbachev pointed out. Hopes are picking up for a possible change for the better in international relations. East-West dialogue, a mechanism which worked so well during the 1970s, is again being set into motion. The Soviet Union was and is for a broad approach to developing this dialogue and using all of its possibilities.

The peaceable goals of Soviet foreign policy were forcefully reaffirmed once again at a recent session of the USSR Supreme Soviet, which approved a plan for the socioeconomic development of the USSR for 1986. The constructive and forward-looking character of the USSR's development stems naturally from the major draft documents of the Twenty-seventh CPSU Congress, which have been published for nationwide discussion.

December 12, 1985

15

A MEETING WITH THE PARTICIPANTS AT THE FORTY–FIRST SESSION OF THE CMEA

MIKHAIL GORBACHEV warmly greeted the participants in the meeting and noted that the Council for Mutual Economic Assistance (CMEA) session was an important event in the life of the socialist community. He highly assessed the work carried out collectively in drafting a comprehensive program for the scientific and technical progress of the CMEA member countries for the period ending in the year 2000.

The socialist system provides bountiful opportunities for scaling the heights of scientific and technological progress. The fullest possible utilization of the advantages of socialism, a rapid buildup of the economic, social and cultural potential of our countries, their technological independence from and invulnerability to pressure and blackmail on the part of imperialism depend on our successes in this sphere. To achieve this, it is necessary to intensify social production on the basis of the latest achievements in science and technology, to pool efforts and to interact more closely in the key areas of cooperation.

The General Secretary of the CPSU Central Committee stressed that the implementation of the comprehensive program will make a valuable contribution to accelerating social and economic development, and enhancing the unity and cohesion of the fraternal countries. This is in line with the general course agreed upon at meetings of their top leaders.

The Communist Party of the Soviet Union regards the implementation of the comprehensive program as a political task of paramount importance for the entire state and the Party. The CPSU Central Committee directs Soviet Communists and economic managers toward the most vigorous participation in the joint work of scientific institutions and enterprises of the countries of the socialist community in the development of modern technology and putting it to use.

The development of twenty-first century technology, Mikhail Gorbachev noted, demands a purposeful attitude and a full scope for creative thinking and initiative. Socialist society has all of these resources. It offers a vast field for innovation, for the manifestation of the talents of all working people, especially young people.

In essence the socialist countries are confronted by qualitatively new tasks. Hence, the organization of work must be approached in a new manner, especially within the framework of the Council for Mutual Economic Assistance.

The comprehensive program accords with the socialist community's common interests. It contains the time-tested principles of equitable and mutually beneficial cooperation. As experience has shown, national tasks are resolved both more quickly and more effectively when the potentials and aims of the whole community are taken into account and when there is reliance on its common potential.

Socialism opposes the technological isolationism and hegemonism characteristic of the major imperialist powers. The comprehensive program provides for active participation in scientific and technological cooperation by all the socialist countries concerned. In pooling their efforts, they certainly do not give up even broader international exchanges in the field of science and technology.

The interest of the socialist countries in working for a lasting and just peace on Earth accords with the aspirations of all peoples. In this connection, emphasis once again was laid on a consistent, purposeful struggle for disarmament and preventing the militarization of outer space, for strengthening international security all over the world and for a practical implementation of the provisions of the Soviet-American statement on the results of the Geneva Summit. Confidence was expressed that the coordinated foreign policy of the fraternal socialist states will further serve as a reliable constructive factor in international politics.

December 18, 1985

16

A MEETING
WITH BERNARD LOWN

MIKHAIL GORBACHEV, General Secretary of the Central Committee of the Communist Party of the Soviet Union, received Professor Bernard Lown, U.S. co-chairman of the International Physicians for the Prevention of Nuclear War (IPPNW), in the Kremlin on December 18, 1985. Academician Yevgeny Chazov, Soviet co-chairman of IPPNW, took part in the meeting.

During the conversation Bernard Lown spoke of the activities of IPPNW, which brings together more than 145,000 physicians and medical workers from more than 50 countries. By studying the possible medical and biological consequences of nuclear war and informing the public, political figures, and governments of the findings, the IPPNW makes a substantial contribution to the cause of preventing nuclear war.

The program being put forward by the IPPNW envisages a freeze, reduction and elimination of nuclear arms, prohibition of nuclear tests, renunciation of a first use of nuclear weapons, nonproliferation of the arms race to outer space and broad international peaceful cooperation.

Bernard Lown emphasized the exceptional importance of drawing broad masses of people into a discussion of the problems of ending the arms race and removing the threat of nuclear war. He said that the voice of the peoples of the world should be heard and should have an effect on governments' decisions.

Mr. Lown highly valued the USSR's peace initiatives, in particular the moratorium on all nuclear explosions, which was put into effect on August 6 of this year. The call to announce such a moratorium was contained in the message of the Fifth International Congress of the IPPNW addressed to Mikhail Gorbachev and to President Ronald Reagan of the United States in the summer of this year. Mr. Lown said that termination of nuclear testing meets the aspirations of all the world's peoples.

Mikhail Gorbachev congratulated Professor Bernard Lown

and Academician Yevgeny Chazov for the award of the Nobel Peace Prize for 1985 to International Physicians for the Prevention of Nuclear War. He said that there exists in the Soviet Union great respect and sympathy for the activities of this movement and for its socially significant life-defending mission. The IPPNW rightfully holds an authoritative place in the world antiwar movement. Doctors reveal the grim truth which people need to know so they can protect that which is irreparable. In this sense the Hippocratic Oath, which obliges physicians to protect their patients against everything that might threaten their lives, assumes a truly new dimension in the nuclear age.

The appeal of the Fifth Congress of this international movement of physicians to the General Secretary of the CPSU Central Committee and to the President of the United States is imbued with the ardent wish to protect all people of Earth against the disastrous consequences of nuclear catastrophe.

Human thought is not always capable of grasping changes of historic scope in time. This is a serious failing, particularly dangerous now that nuclear holocaust directly threatens every home and every family. So the voice of the peoples of the world and of their public organizations in defense of peace is all the more important now. This is a kind of expression of the instinct of humankind's self-preservation.

Peace based on deterrence by means of nuclear weapons is a precarious one. It is impossible to consolidate peace through an arms buildup and space arms. No one has yet invented a more reliable and effective model of relations among states than détente and cooperation under conditions of peace and mutual security. The lowering of the level of military confrontation among them would consolidate the framework of these relations, making them stable and reliable.

Proceeding from these factors, we agreed to a meeting between the Soviet and American leaders in Geneva, said Mikhail Gorbachev. In the course of the meeting an important beginning was made in the normalization of Soviet-American relations and preconditions were created for the improvement of the international situation as a whole.

However, we see another thing as well: Reactionary, aggression-minded circles in the U.S., which some time ago tried hard to disrupt the Geneva meeting, are now attacking its results. A broad campaign has been launched against the normalization of relations with the USSR and against the consolidation of mutual trust in Soviet-American relations to which the sides agreed in Geneva. Propaganda in the press, television and cinema are being actively used for fanning mistrust and hostility toward the USSR and the Soviet people. The impression is that there are people in the U.S. for whom the desire to improve mutual understanding between our peoples as expressed in Geneva is very much in the way. By all appearances, the notorious "hawks" have set themselves the task of preventing the implementation of the Geneva Accords and of disrupting or at least lessening the importance of another Soviet-American summit meeting. Unfortunately, the latest statements of U.S. statesmen as well are at variance with the "spirit of Geneva."

As for the Soviet Union, its policy is clear and consistent. The Soviet Union is prepared to go its part of the road toward the construction of a structure of durable mutual security and peaceful cooperation with the United States. But we expect the same from the U.S. leadership. We extended a hand to the United States in Geneva. We are prepared to pass from competition in armaments to disarmament, from confrontation to cooperation. "Cooperation, not confrontation" was the slogan of the recent International Congress of the Physicians for the Prevention of Nuclear War. One cannot but agree with this. Cooperation is nowadays the indispensable condition for both the progress of our civilization and of our common survival.

The Soviet Union will go as far as is needed toward the complete elimination of nuclear weapons and toward the ultimate removal of the threat of war with their use. We are in favor of really ensuring humanity's primary right, the right to live. We are for the immediate freezing of nuclear arms, for a complete ban of nuclear tests without time-limit, for the most effective control of these weapons. Reciprocity is our only condition.

As a real major step on the way to universal nuclear disarmament we proposed to the United States a radical fifty per cent reduction of strategic nuclear arsenals with, of course, a complete ban on space strike arms. This means the renunciation of the "Star Wars" program, a program which can only destroy all efforts at the elimination of nuclear arms and whip up the arms race to unprecedented proportions. As it is justly noted in the appeal of the physicians' movement, the threat of global nuclear conflict would increase sharply as a result of "Star Wars."

Actually, this is understood now by the whole world. As many as 151 states, in fact all the United Nations member countries except for the United States, just voted for the resolution of the United Nations General Assembly on the prevention of the arms race in outer space.

Mikhail Gorbachev especially touched upon the question of ending the tests of nuclear weapons, called for persistently by the IPPNW, which substantiates its call with convincing reasons. The moratorium on all nuclear explosions, announced by the Soviet Union as of August 6 of this year, has been highly appreciated in the world. "Making this step, we proceeded from a sincere desire to break the vicious circle: To stop the endless sophistication of nuclear weapons and steer matters to an actual immobilization of their stocks. I told this to President Reagan in Geneva," Mikhail Gorbachev said. "To our profound regret, the United States has not up to now followed our example."

In reply to Bernard Lown, Mikhail Gorbachev said: "We are ready to extend the USSR-introduced moratorium on nuclear explosions if the United States reciprocates. We are urging the U.S. Administration to do that. A unique chance is still there to make the moratorium mutual and to extend it beyond January 1. To miss this chance, which paves the way to a final ban in treaty form on all tests of nuclear weapons would be unreasonable, to say the least. A solution to this question is in the hands of the U.S. Government.

"Professor Lown is right: The people of the world are waiting for the termination and prohibition of the tests of nuclear weapons without delay. This is also indicated by a resolution to that effect, which was recently passed, practically unanimously, by the UN General Assembly (with three negative votes—those of the United States, Great Britain, and France)."

In conclusion, Mikhail Gorbachev wished his interlocutors and all the members of International Physicians for the Prevention of Nuclear War new successes in their highly necessary and lofty activities.

Page 1

On the way to a private talk. Geneva, November 19, 1985.

Page 2

Soviet Minister of Foreign Affairs Eduard Shevardnadze and U.S. Secretary of State George Shultz sign bilateral Agreement on Exchanges and Contacts in Science, Education and Culture in the presence of Mikhail Gorbachev and Ronald Reagan. Geneva, November 21, 1985.

Page 3, top photo

Mikhail Gorbachev talks with Bernard Lown, U.S. Co-Chairman of the International Physicians for the Prevention of Nuclear War. The Kremlin, December 18, 1985.

Page 3, bottom photo:

Mikhail Gorbachev visits a synthetic textile factory in Kustanai (Kazakh Soviet Socialist Republic, Central Asia).

Page 4, top photo

Greeting a group of workers famous for their skill and innovations. The Kremlin, September 20, 1985.

Page 4, bottom photo

Mikhail Gorbachev welcomes Malcolm Baldridge, U.S. Secretary of Commerce in the Kremlin. December 10, 1985.

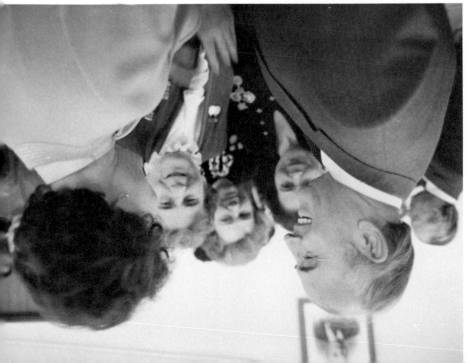

17

AN ADDRESS TO
THE DIPLOMATIC MISSIONS
IN THE KREMLIN

$\mathbf{B}$EFORE THE START of the new year let me wholeheartedly greet here, in the Kremlin, the heads of the diplomatic missions of foreign states accredited in the Soviet Union.

I greet the representatives of the socialist states with which we are tied by bonds of fraternal friendship and close cooperation in carrying out the outlined programs of socialist and communist construction, in speeding up the social and economic development of our societies and in joint efforts for a lasting peace on Earth.

I greet the representatives of states which have freed themselves of colonial oppression and embarked on the path of independent development, the member states of the nonaligned movement. Our relations with these states are those of sincere friendship, mutual respect and multifaceted cooperation. We consider it a good augury of history that the role of the nonaligned states on the world scene has been growing steadily.

I greet the representatives of a different, capitalist social system present in this hall, the representatives of the states of North America, Western Europe, the Far East and other regions, which belong to the category of countries which it is customary in modern political language to call the West. The Soviet Union consistently seeks to build its relations with these countries on the basis of the principles of peaceful coexistence and equitable mutually beneficial cooperation. We are well aware that prospects for universal peace are dependent to a considerable extent on the state of our relations with this group of states, and we approach this issue with a keen sense of responsibility.

Dear Comrades and Gentlemen,

We are at a threshold which does not simply mark the succession of one year by another according to the calendar but also has another, much more profound meaning.

The year 1985 has been packed with events of major historical significance. Some of them spell new and formidable dangers to humanity, while others inspire hope. It depends on the activities of people—governments, statesmen, politicians and the world public at large—which of these two trends will prevail in the coming year of 1986; whether it will become a year of real action to strengthen peace and international security and develop peaceful intercourse and cooperation among nations or whether the threat of a nuclear catastrophe, which has come to loom large over the planet, will become still greater.

The dangers are obvious. They include an ongoing, runaway arms race and stubborn attempts by militarist quarters to extend it to outer space. They include flagrant violations of the independence and sovereignty of a number of states and outside interference in the domestic affairs of nations. But it is also obvious that these processes have encountered mounting resistance the world over. And, I may say, they have added to the responsibility of all states and peoples for the destiny of universal peace.

Each people, each country, big, middle-sized or small, can contribute grains of its national experience to the cause of peace and international cooperation. This has been confirmed once again by the just-ended session of the UN General Assembly, which has taken, practically by consensus, a number of very important decisions, including those on the prevention of an arms race in outer space and on putting an end to nuclear weapons tests.

So far as the Soviet leadership is concerned, by our convictions we are optimists. We believe in a better future for humanity and will continue making vigorous efforts in this direction.

There has been an exchange of signals between East and West of late, which has opened up some hope—I would put it even more cautiously, a gleam of hope—for moving forward to mutually acceptable solutions.

As a result of the Soviet-U.S. meeting in Geneva, there has taken place, as is now widely recognized, a certain warming-up of the international climate. There have also emerged certain points of contiguity (or rather yet potential contiguity) on problems covered by the talks on nuclear and space arms. How things will work out there depends first of all on how the accord reached at the summit meeting in Geneva will flesh out in practice. It will depend on the progress of these talks whether 1986 will justify the peoples' hope for the prevention of an arms race in space and its termination on Earth.

Thanks to constructive efforts by a number of states, the outlines of possible agreements at the Stockholm Conference on Confidence and Security-Building Measures and Disarmament in Europe appear to be taking shape. All its participants must, in our view, work with their sleeves rolled up to achieve positive results at Stockholm before the next All-European meeting slated for next fall.

The wish of the sides to reckon with each other's interests and concerns is more noticeable at the Vienna talks on the reduction of armed forces and armaments in Central Europe. We are now carefully studying the latest proposals of the western partners.

It seems that the participants in the Geneva Disarmament Conference began realizing better the urgent need to ban chemical weapons, to end all nuclear tests and exclude the use of force in outer space. But serious efforts will yet be necessary. The USSR is ready to go its part of the way toward balanced agreements.

The question of nuclear explosions is now the focus of attention of statesmen and the broad public. These explosions have rocked the Earth for several decades now. It is time to put an end to that. We are convinced that this is within the realm of the possible.

We have urged and continue urging the USA to follow the Soviet Union's good example and end all nuclear explosions. Should the two biggest powers come out jointly on this issue of such great importance for all humanity, this would be a step of a truly outstanding significance.

In your persons, esteemed diplomatic representatives, I am addressing all states and peoples: Let us act so that the year 1986 shall go down in history as a year of a decline in nuclear explosions and as a year when people have found enough common sense to rise above narrow, selfish motives and stop doing harm to their own planet.

Since references are often made to the so-called verification problem as a pretext for evading a resolution of that issue, I will stress once again most definitely that this problem will not be a stumbling block as far as the Soviet Union is concerned. The Soviet Union is prepared to take most resolute steps toward on-site inspection as regards verification of the ending of nuclear testing.

Our country, which has learned from its bitter experience what a perfidious attack is, has a stake in reliable and rigorous verification no less than anyone else. Under present-day international conditions, given the deficit of mutual trust, verification measures are simply indispensable. Let it be verification by the use of national technical means, or international verification. The main thing is that it be verification of compliance with concrete agreements.

The Soviet leadership is ready to reach agreement on a sensible and fair basis and would like to hope for a realistic and serious approach also on the part of its partners. The soil of the reconvening talks should be sown even today with good seeds, since only they can ensure good young growth in spring and a crop in autumn.

There is yet another major and acute problem. The Soviet Union is firmly set on seeing substantial progress in 1986 in the political settlements in the Middle East, Central America, around Afghanistan, in southern Africa and in the Persian Gulf area. We are prepared to search for just solutions jointly with other countries and participate, where necessary, in appropriate guarantees.

The habit of looking at conflict situations through the spectacles of East-West political or ideological confrontation is detrimental to the striving to eliminate trouble spots and, at any rate, to prevent them from growing. It is shortsighted and dangerous to build policy on erroneous concepts. Conflicts grow out of the local social, economic and political soil. Hence they should be resolved in such a way as not to infringe upon the legitimate interests of the peoples of the world, their right to choose, without interference from the outside, the way of life they wish, as well as the right to protect their choice.

Our esteemed guests, I would like to stress in conclusion how great the role of diplomatic representatives is at this crucial juncture. The decisions taken by the leadership of the respective countries depend to no small degree on the completeness and trustworthiness of the evaluations and information of these diplomats. In general, it will be perhaps no exaggeration to say that trust between states starts with ambassadors. I would add that we demand full objectivity and an unbiased attitude from our ambassadors.

For our part, we want you to be well informed about what is going on in the Soviet Union, and certainly not only in the capital. The Soviet authorities will further accord hospitality and give assistance to the foreign ambassadors in this. We have nothing to conceal: The plans and intentions of the Soviet people, of the Soviet leadership, are peaceful and only peaceful.

You are certainly aware of what place the upcoming Twenty-seventh Congress of the Communist Party of the Soviet Union occupies in the life of our Party and of our whole country. Many, I hope, have familiarized themselves with the theoretical and political documents being presented to the Congress—the new edition of the CPSU Program, the changes in the party charter and the Guidelines for the Economic and Social Development of the USSR in 1986-1990 and the Period up to the Year 2000. We are looking even farther, into the Third Millennium, as regards many parameters.

What it is going to be depends in no small measure on the present generation.

All have an enormous responsibility to bear today. The point is to use the possibility, which has opened, to reduce the quantities of weapons, to prevent the monstrous danger stemming from outer space and make, on the whole, our beautiful world a place worthy of human beings.

On behalf of all my compatriots, who are meeting the new

year in a good, joyful and creative mood, I wish peace and well-being to the peoples of all countries, which you represent, the peoples of the whole world. I wish success and personal happiness to you and your families, esteemed guests, the personnel of the embassies you head, representatives of foreign trade offices, banks and firms, journalists and technical specialists, lecturers and students, in a word, all citizens of your countries living and working in the Soviet Union.

December 27, 1985

18

A REPLY TO
KENNETH LIVINGSTONE

Dear Mr. Livingstone,*

I read your appeal with close attention, pervaded with awareness of the need to take urgent measures to rid the world's peoples of the nuclear threat. The worry of your compatriots about the dangerous development of the world situation is fully shared in the Soviet Union.

Humanity is living through a critical period of its history. It has no choice but to survive or to destroy itself entirely. So today it is more incumbent than ever before upon all the politicians to whom people have entrusted responsibility for their future to display a broad statesmanlike approach and the ability to rise above narrow, selfish interests and to realize in full the collective and individual responsibility of states for the destinies of peace.

Following its clear and consistently peaceable course, the Soviet Union is doing everything it can to close the door to weapons in space and to achieve radical reductions in nuclear armaments and their eventual complete elimination. And the Soviet Union does take positive steps in this direction, the need for which you point out in your appeal. The USSR has already assumed the obligation not to be the first to use nuclear weapons and has introduced a unilateral moratorium on all nuclear explosions. It now depends on the U.S. Government to realize the prospect of its becoming a mutual agreement.

We stand for the immediate freezing of nuclear armaments and for the complete prohibition of their tests in perpetuity, moreover, with most effective control. We are prepared again to

---

*Kenneth Livingstone, leader of the Greater London Council, which governs the British capital, sent a letter to Mikhail Gorbachev, General Secretary of the Central Committee of the Communist Party of the Soviet Union, in December 1985, presenting views of British campaigners for the establishment of nuclear-weapon-free zones. (The Greater London Council proclaimed the city a nuclear-free zone on July 21, 1981.) The letter outlines the goals of the movement and stresses that there has never been a stronger need for the progress of international disarmament talks than there is today.

The leader of the Greater London Council voiced support for the steps taken to lessen the risk of nuclear war, including those already taken by the Soviet Union.

sit down to the negotiating table in the immediate future to find jointly with representatives of the USA and Great Britain a mutually acceptable solution to this problem.

You also know that our country suggested that the corresponding nuclear armaments of the USSR and the USA be halved. Naturally, progress at the Geneva talks is only possible if space strike armaments are completely prohibited, in other words, if the "Star Wars" program is renounced, because its implementation could lead to strategic chaos and to a qualitatively new, uncontrollable round of the arms race. Regrettably, we see that the ruinous consequences of involvement in the "Star Wars" plans have not yet been realized in full by the ruling circles of either Great Britain or some other of the United States' closest allies.

I recollect with warmth my visit to your country a year ago and numerous meetings on British soil. I understand why Britons strive to preserve their traditions and historical heritage, to add to their achievements in different fields and to hand all of this down to their descendants intact and in full.

Similar concern is displayed by people in other European countries, in the Soviet Union, actually, the world over. This is why the anxiety of the people of the world over the fact that the ever growing heaps of deadly weapons are blocking the way to the implementation of these noble, humanitarian tasks is well justified. Today even the comparatively small British Isles are being stuffed with nuclear weapons whose presence, it should be admitted openly, does not consolidate anybody's security.

Measures aimed at the nonproliferation of nuclear weapons and the creation of nuclear-free zones in various parts of the world hold an important place in the struggle for the reduction of the sphere of nuclear preparations. The proclamation of separate areas and cities to be nuclear-free zones is developing in the same direction. We regard it as a sign showing that the world's peoples are realizing their responsibility for the destinies of the world and are going to act in ways that are within their capacity. The building of peace is being created out of separate bricks. The capital of détente is being accumulated by grains.

It is gratifying to see that the movement of municipal councils and other organizations in support for the creation of nuclear-free zones is expanding and graining in strength. In our opinion, the creation of such zones is not merely a good wish or an idealistic dream. It is a positive phenomenon of international life reflecting the will of ordinary people for peace, cooperation and détente.

In our attitude to nuclear-free zones we do not make exceptions for any countries, no matter if they are members of military alliances or not. There is only one condition for us: If this or that country refuses to acquire nuclear weapons and does not have them on its territory, it receives from us firm and effective guarantees. For example, if Great Britain fully rejected nuclear weapons and dismantled foreign nuclear bases on its territory, the USSR would guarantee that the Soviet nuclear weapons will be neither trained on British territory, nor used against it. These guarantees could be legalized through concluding an official agreement that would take into account all the corresponding military aspects.

We highly appreciate the striving of the Greater London Council, just as that of hundreds of other municipal councils in dozens of the countries of the world, to make a contribution to the common efforts of the peoples of the world aimed at removing the nuclear threat and reviving an atmosphere of trust and mutual understanding in relations among states.

I wish you fresh success in your noble activities for continued world peace. Please accept my best wishes for the next year.

Mikhail Gorbachev
January 3, 1986

19

A MESSAGE
TO THE PARTICIPANTS
IN THE CONGRESS FOR
A PEACEFUL FUTURE
OF THE PLANET

I GREET the participants in the Congress of Scientists and Prominent Figures in Culture for a Peaceful Future of the Planet.

Your Congress opens the calendar of tangible actions which will certainly abound in 1986, which has been declared by the United Nations Organization the International Year of Peace. It is significant that you have gathered in Warsaw, a city whose past reminds one of the horrors of the last war and whose present-day appearance symbolizes humanity's irresistible will for constructive endeavor and peace.

Humanity today is facing quite a few complex and difficult problems at national, regional and global levels. But there is not one more urgent among them than the task of removing the nuclear threat—stopping the arms race on Earth and preventing it from spreading to outer space—and preserving civilization.

The Soviet-U.S. meeting in Geneva has kindled hope for improvements in the international situation and stronger mutual security. To have this hope materialized, it is essential that both sides fulfill the accords reached in good faith. The Geneva process should be carried on and determine the further course of events in the world. This is demanded by the peoples and is really necessary.

I can assure the delegates to the Congress that the Soviet Union will continue to do its best to curb the arms race, to terminate it on Earth and prevent it in outer space. This is what our far-reaching steps, plans and proposals are aimed at, coming into line with the interests of further progress of all humankind. Our choice is not military competition, but comprehensive international cooperation in all spheres, including the sphere of science and culture.

In a bid to assist to a maximum degree a radical improvement of the international situation and the ridding of the human race, once and for all, of the fear of the possibility of a nuclear holocaust or use of other barbaric weapons of mass annihilation, the Soviet Union has just advanced a peace initiative of historic significance addressed to the United States of America, the other nuclear powers and to all governments and nations of the world.

We propose reaching agreement on the adoption of a program for the complete elimination of nuclear weapons the world over within the next fifteen years, before the end of the twentieth century. We put forward a concrete plan of step-by-step measures leading toward that goal and provide for strict international verification of their implementation. We are convinced that this is a realistic prospect, naturally on the condition that the development of space strike weapons is renounced. The atom only for peace, outer space only for peace—this is our program.

We also propose to eliminate, as early as in this century, chemical weapons, their stockpiles and the industrial base for their manufacture—also under strict verification, including international on-site inspections.

We suggest banning the development of non-nuclear arms based on new physical principles and approaching nuclear and other weapons of mass destruction in their hitting power.

We also consider it possible to reach, at long last, meaningful accords on mutual troop and arms reductions in the center of Europe at the Vienna talks and on non-use of force and strengthening mutual confidence at the conference in Stockholm.

As one more confirmation of the seriousness and sincerity of its intentions and of its readiness to go over as soon as possible to practical actions for strengthening peace and ridding mankind of the threat of nuclear war, the Soviet Union has decided to prolong for another three months the moratorium it declared on any nuclear explosions and urges the United States and then other nuclear powers to accede to it.

In short, the Soviet Union comes up with a concrete program for achieving the aim to which your Congress is devoted, the aim of safeguarding a peaceful future for this planet. And we appeal to the peace forces throughout the world to support this program.

We are convinced that mankind's intellectual potential

should be used for amplifying its material and cultural riches and not for developing new types of deadly weapons of global destruction. Peaceful cooperation of states and peoples, and not preparation for "Star Wars"—such is the way we understand humanity's approach to the question of space. Peaceful space is an important precondition for banishing the danger of war from the lives of people.

The great power of the struggle for peace lies in words of truth, truth about the terrible consequences of a nuclear conflict unless it is averted. The participants at your Congress—influential representatives of scientific and cultural communities—can play a significant role in disseminating this truth and making broad public circles aware of their humane duty to take an active part in efforts for a really lasting peace.

I wish your Congress success in its work toward the common aim which is the main one for all—the triumph of a durable peace on Earth.

Mikhail Gorbachev
January 17, 1986

20

TO THE PARTICIPANTS IN A SUMMIT MEETING OF SIX EAST AFRICAN LEADERS

I CORDIALLY greet the participants in a meeting of the heads of states and governments of six East African countries, who assembled to set up an intergovernmental organization charged with the task of combatting drought and promoting economic development in the region.

Being firmly committed to developing equitable and mutually beneficial inter-state cooperation and also loyal to friendship with the newly-free countries, the Soviet Union supports the striving by your states to pool efforts to resolve complex socio-economic and ecological problems.

We hope that constructive interaction of East African states in the aforementioned area will serve the benefit of their peoples and become one of the factors in promoting mutual understanding and peace in the region. We also hope it will contribute to further consolidation of the potential of all forces in the world advocating social progress, which are against colonialism, neo-colonialism and racism, and for the establishment of a new, more just international economic order, for the removal of the military threat and improvement of the international political and economic climate.

I wish your meeting successful and fruitful work.

January 15, 1986

PART II
DOMESTIC POLICY

21

A REPORT TO
THE PLENARY MEETING
OF THE CPSU CENTRAL
COMMITTEE
ON CONVENING
THE 27TH CPSU CONGRESS

COMRADES,

Our Party, the Soviet people and the peoples of the socialist countries and all progressive mankind solemnly marked yesterday as the 115th anniversary of the birth of Vladimir Ilyich Lenin.

Life itself and the entire course of history convincingly confirm the great truth of Lenin's teaching. It has been and remains for us a guide to action, a source of inspiration, and a reliable compass for determining the strategy and tactics of our march forward.

Lenin taught Communists to proceed, in everything, from the working people's interests, to make a profound study of realities, to assess social phenomena realistically from class positions, and to be in a constant creative quest for the best ways of implementing the ideals of Communism.

Today we compare our actions and plans with what Lenin taught, with his great ideas, and we live and work according to Lenin's behests.

Our Plenary Meeting is to consider questions of great political importance—the convening of the Twenty-seventh Party Congress and the tasks involved in preparing and holding it.

The Politburo proposes, in keeping with the Rules of the CPSU, that the next Party Congress be convened on February 25, 1986. It proposes that the Congress agenda include the following items:

1. Report by the CPSU Central Committee and the tasks of the Party.
2. Report by the CPSU Central Auditing Commission.
3. On redrafting the CPSU Program.
4. On changes in the CPSU Rules.
5. On the Guidelines for the Economic and Social Development of the USSR for 1986-1990 and for the Period Ending in the Year 2000.
6. Election of the Party's central bodies.

It is intended to hear and discuss the reviews on the reports by the CPSU Central Committee and the Central Auditing Commission of the CPSU, and also on the Guidelines for economic and social development. As for the redrafted Program and changes in the CPSU Rules, they can be dealt with in the Central Committee Report and it is not necessary to present separate reports on them.

It is proposed that one out of every 3,670 Communists be elected a delegate to the Congress. So there will be altogether 5,000 delegates. This will make it possible to have all the organizations of our Party fully represented and to reflect the Party's social and national composition.

In the ten months left before the opening of the Congress, we should make an all-round analysis and a realistic assessment of what has been done since the Twenty-sixth Congress and to determine the prospects for further development and the tasks of home and foreign policy. We should prepare extremely important documents and, above all, such fundamental documents as the redrafted CPSU Program and the Guidelines for development for the next five-year period and until the end of the century, to consider them at a Plenary Meeting of the CPSU Central Committee, and then submit them for broad discussion by the Party and the whole country. Great attention should be paid to the drawing up of reports and holding of elections at a high level by Party organizations and to the fulfilling of the targets of the Eleventh Five-Year Plan in a fitting manner.

In short, it will be a period of intensive and versatile work—political, economic, organizational and ideological-theoretical.

Today, we once again affirm the continuity of the strategic line worked out by the Twenty-sixth Party Congress and the subsequent Plenary Meetings of the Central Committee. Continuity, as Lenin understood it, means steady advance, the singling out and solution of new problems and elimination of everything that hinders development. We must follow this Leninist tradition unswervingly and enrich and develop our Party policy and our general line of perfecting developed socialist society.

The forthcoming Twenty-seventh CPSU Congress will undoubtedly become a landmark in the country's development. Its importance is determined by the paramount significance of the questions put on the agenda, the characteristic features of the current period and the novelty and scope of the tasks facing society. This imparts a special significance to the entire pre-Congress work of the Party and calls for a profound understanding of the current situation as well as bold decisions and vigorous actions.

The country has achieved major successes in all spheres of public life. Relying on the advantages offered by the new system, it has, within a historically short period of time, attained summits of economic and social progress. Today the USSR has a powerful, highly-developed economy and skilled work force, specialists and research personnel. We lead the world in many fields of industry, science and technology.

There have been profound changes in social life. For the first time in history the working man has become the master of his country, the maker of his own destiny. The guaranteed right to work and remuneration for work, society's concern for man from his birth to old age, wide access to intellectual culture, respect for the dignity and rights of the individual, the steady broadening of the working people's participation in management—all these are permanent values and inherent features of the socialist way of life. Herein lies the most important source of political stability, social optimism and confidence in the future.

The Soviet people are justly proud of all this. But life and its dynamism dictate the need for further changes and transformations, for bringing about a qualitatively new state of society, in the broadest sense of the word. This means, first of all, the modernization of production of the basis of scientific and technological achievements and the attainment of the world's highest level of labor productivity. This also means the perfection of social relations and, above all, economic relations. This means major changes in the sphere of work and in the material and cultural standards of the people. This means an invigoration of the entire system of political and social institutions, the extension of socialist democracy and people's self-government.

The development of Soviet society will be largely determined by qualitative changes in the economy, by its going over the intensive methods of development and by a maximum rise in efficiency. The state of the national economy should be assessed, and future tasks determined, precisely from these positions.

As is well known, alongside the successes achieved in the country's economic development, unfavorable trends have grown in the last few years and quite a few difficulties have arisen. We managed to improve the work of many sectors of the national economy and to improve the situation somewhat, thanks to the active work carried out by the Party, beginning from 1983. However, the difficulties are far from being completely overcome and much effort needs to be made in order to build a reliable foundation for achieving rapid progress.

What is the reason for the difficulties? The answer to this question, as you no doubt realize, is a matter of fundamental importance for the Party.

Of course, the influence of natural and a number of external factors has made itself felt. But the main thing, I believe, is that the changes in the objective conditions of industrial development and the need for accelerating its intensification and for introducing changes in the methods of economic management were not properly taken into consideration in good time and, what is especially important, no persistent efforts were made to elaborate and implement large-scale measures in the economic sphere.

We must, Comrades, fully and profoundly grasp the situation that has taken shape and draw some basic conclusions. The country's historic destiny and the positions of Socialism in the world today in a large measure depend on how we shall act further. By using on a wide scale the achievements of scientific and technological evolution, and by devising forms of socialist economic management in keeping with modern conditions and requirements, we shall achieve a substantial acceleration of socioeconomic progress. There is simply no other way.

This is what determines today the success of the cause of Socialism and Communism and the tremendous responsibility that rests with the Party, its Central Committee and all Party organizations at the current, most important period of history. And we Communists must do everything to live up to this responsibility and to the major tasks which are dictated by our times.

The main question now is how and with what resources will the country be able to accelerate economic development? Considering this question in the Politburo, we have unanimously arrived at the conclusion that real possibilities for this exist. The task of accelerating the rates of growth, and a substantial growth at that, is quite feasible if we place at the focus of all our work the intensification of the economy and acceleration of scientific and technological progress, if we carry out a reorganization of management, planning and the structural and investment policy, if we raise the efficiency of organization and strengthen discipline everywhere and if we basically improve the style of our work.

I think that participants in the Plenary Meeting will support this conclusion.

It is possible to obtain relatively quick results if we put organizational-economic and social reserves to work and above all if we activate the human factor, i.e. make sure that every person works on his job conscientiously and to the best of his ability.

How great are the possibilities that exist in this respect was noted at the recent meeting with workers, managers, specialists and scientists at the CPSU Central Committee. When the need arises, the participants in this meeting pointed out, it is possible to raise labor productivity within a short time to such a degree that it may at times be comparable to the planned targets for an entire five-year period because the collectives and their leaders brace up and start to work better.

And such reserves can be found at every enterprise, every construction site and every collective and state farm. Nobody knows better about them than the work collectives themselves, their Party organizations and managers. Therefore, much depends on their approach to work, on their activity and their ability to get people interested in the maximal utilization of all existing possibilities for increasing production and raising its efficiency.

An important aspect of the question of responsibility and discipline is the timely and efficient deliveries of raw materials, fuel, finished articles, containers, etc. There are people who are responsible for this and who should be made answerable for this. Some progress has been made in the strengthening of contractual discipline in the national economy. It must be consolidated by steadily increasing exactingness in the matter of the fulfillment of contractual obligations without making any allowances for objective conditions.

Another source of reserves which should definitely be used is the struggle against waste and losses. Executives in many ministries and enterprises try to get as much capital investments, machine-tools, machinery, raw materials and fuel as possible from the state. But their approach to the matter of rational utilization of resources is quite often irresponsible. Equipment sometimes stays idle or is not used to the full.

And how do matters stand in capital construction? The construction of many projects is taking an unreasonably long time. As a result, quite a lot of material resources are left unused. The expansion of capacities is being held up and the country does not get the products it needs in time.

The plan for putting into operation fixed productive assets is not being fulfilled satisfactorily. A good deal of equipment has not been installed as planned, but has been accumulating at depots of enterprises and construction sites. The direct losses of material values are quite considerable because of negligence in the haulage, storage and use of cement, coal, mineral fertilizers, timber, agricultural produce and foodstuffs.

We must put an end to such waste immediately. It is obviously not enough to issue appeals only—there have been plenty of them. It is necessary to make persons who are responsible for the proper storage and correct utilization of all material values more strictly answerable, legally answerable for their work. Good order must be established at every enterprise and construction site, at every collective and state farm, at every organization. Without this there can be no talk about any kind of rational economic management or the growth of the economy's efficiency.

The Party attaches foremost importance to the task of greatly accelerating scientific and technological progress as the key strategic level of intensification of the national economy and the most rational utilization of the accumulated potential. A special meeting of the CPSU Central Committee is scheduled for June to discuss this question. Here I would like to make some observations that are of fundamental importance.

In most sectors scientific and technological progress is taking place at a sluggish pace, in fact, evolutionally, as it were, mostly through improving existing technology and in part through modernizing machines and equipment. Implementation of these measures, of course, does give certain results, but only small ones. There should be revolutionary changes, a transfer to fundamentally new technological systems, to technologies of the latest generations, which ensure the highest efficiency. This means in fact a retooling of all the sectors of the national economy on the basis of up-to-date achievements of science and technology.

The urgency of the question is explained by the fact that over the last years the country's production facilities have aged considerably, and the rate of renewal of the fixed productive assets has dropped. That is why the task of considerably increasing the rate of replacement of equipment should be given priority in the Twelfth five-year plan period.

The machine-building industry has a decisive role to play here. Its development should be given priority so that the industry's growth rate would be 1.5 to 2 times higher in the Twelfth five-year plan period. The key task is to go quickly over to the production of new generations of machines and equipment which can ensure the introduction of progressive technology, raise productivity several times over, reduce the amount of material required per unit of output and increase the returns on assets. Priority should be given to the machine-tool manufacturing industry and to accelerating the development of computer technology, instrument-making, electrical engineering and electronics as catalysts of scientific and technological progress.

In the light of these tasks one cannot regard as normal the fall in the prestige of the work of the engineer. There is room for improvement here. We must enhance the role and prestige of foremen, engineers, designers and technologists and provide greater material and moral incentives for their work.

The acceleration of scientific and technological progress and the growth of production efficiency are inseparable from a decisive improvement in output quality. The goods produced fail to meet modern technological, economic, aesthetic and, for that matter, all consumer requirements. They are sometimes of obviously inferior quality, which is actually plunder of material resources and waste of our people's labor effort. That is why a general rise in the quality of products should be given a central place in our economic policy. Quality and once again quality—this is our motto today. In solving the problem of quality one can at the same time solve the problem of quantity. This is the only reliable way of satisfying on an increasing scale the country's requirements in modern technology and the growing demand of the population for various consumer goods and of eliminating goods shortages in the national economy.

Whatever question we consider, and from whatever point of view we approach the economy, everything finally comes down to the need for a substantial improvement of management and of the economic mechanism as a whole. This was confirmed once again during the recent meeting at the CPSU Central Committee with workers and managers and during the visit to the ZIL Auto Plant. Participants in the meetings were obviously concerned and worried as they described the worsened conditions of work due to flaws in the system of management, unnecessary regimentation and the issuing of superfluous instructions. There is only one way out: Immediate and vigorous measures should be taken covering the whole spectrum of management problems.

Today we have a clearer idea of how the economic mechanism should be restructured. In further developing the principle of centralization in coping with strategic tasks it is necessary to move forward more boldly along the path of broadening the rights of enterprises and their independence, of going over to the cost-accounting system and on this basis to increase the responsibility and interest of work collectives in the end results of their work.

It seems that the results of the large-scale experiment carried out along this line are not bad. But they cannot fully satisfy us. A stage has been reached when we should go over from experiments to setting up an integrated system of economic management. This means that a practical reorganization of work should also be carried out among the upper echelons of economic management, that they should be primarily geared to tackling long-range socioeconomic, scientific and technological tasks and to conducting a search for the most effective forms of uniting science with production.

Today greater demands are being made on planning, which lies at the heart of management. Planning should become an active lever for intensifying production, implementing progressive economic decisions and ensuring a balanced and dynamic growth of the economy. At the same time, the plans drawn up by amalgamations and enterprises should discard some of the many indicators. They should make wider use of economic norms that make for greater initiative and enterprise.

It is time to start streamlining the organizational structures of management, to do away with unnecessary management bodies, to simplify the apparatus and raise its efficiency. It is also important to do this because some of these bodies have become a hindrance to progress. The number of instructions and regulations which at times arbitrarily interpret Party and Government decisions and thus shackle the independence of enterprises should be drastically reduced.

It is extremely important to explain to every work collective and every individual worker the principles of the cost-accounting system. This will make it possible to link up the measures for improving the system of management at the top with the development at a grass-roots level of collective forms of organization and a provision of incentives for work. It will also heighten the activity of working people.

It is no less important to increase the responsibility of republic and local bodies for the supervision of economic, social and cultural work and for meeting the needs of working people. But to do this, it is of course necessary further to extend the rights of local bodies, to enhance their initiative and interest in the development of production, in the rational utilization of resources and the smooth functioning of all spheres of services to the population. Therefore, local authorities should be made fully responsible for dealing with all questions within their competence and should more quickly rid themselves of dependent attitudes.

Comrades, the CPSU regards as the highest purpose of accelerating the country's socioeconomic development a steady, step-by-step improvement of the people's well-being, an improvement of all aspects of their life, and the creation of favorable conditions for the harmonious development of the individual. In this respect it is necessary to consistently pursue a policy aimed at a fairer distribution of material and cultural benefits, at enhancing the influence of social factors on the development of the economy and raising its efficiency.

This policy is meeting with the full approval and support of the Soviet people. What needs to be done now is to work out concrete and effective measures of eliminating from the distribution mechanism the practice of levelling, unearned incomes, and everything that runs counter to the economic norms and moral ideals of our society, and ensuring that the material position of each worker and each work collective should depend directly on the results of their work. The Party will continue to wage a most resolute struggle against all negative phenomena, phenomena that are alien to the socialist way of life and to our communist morals.

Careful drafting of the social program to be presented by the Party at the Twenty-seventh Congress is now under way. At the same time there are urgent tasks that call for special attention.

I refer primarily to the implementation of the Food Program. In recent years, positive changes have taken place in the development of agriculture, and the supply of foodstuffs to the population has somewhat improved. But it still leaves much to be desired. Collective and state farms, as well as the processing enterprises, are in a position to markedly increase the output of foodstuffs. The available possibilities should be employed intelligently and the available potential effectively put to use.

Sometimes attempts are made by local authorities to shift all responsibility concerning food supply, and especially fodder supply, to the central authorities. Such practices are unacceptable. The task is to make the most of all reserves for increasing food production at collective and state farms, and on individual citizens' small-holdings and enterprises' subsidiary farms.

So, Comrades, we ought to step up our work on fulfilling the Food Program and to supplement it with substantial measures aimed at developing the processing branches of the agroindustrial complex and forging closer links between them and collective and state farms. The USSR State Planning Committee and relevant ministries have been assigned these tasks by the Politburo, and they are expected to fulfill them conscientiously and thoroughly.

Management of the agroindustrial complex also needs to be further improved. Far from everything has been done in this respect. Concerned about departmental interests, district and regional associations very often fail to achieve an adequate degree of coordination in solving problems of the comprehensive development of agriculture and related industries. If we are firmly convinced that there should be one master on the land, and that agroindustrial associations should bear full responsibility for the fulfillment of the Food Program (and I hope nobody has doubts on this matter), we must take steps to make it possible to manage, plan and finance the agroindustrial complex as a whole at all levels. This was agreed upon at the May 1982 Plenary Meeting of the CPSU Central Committee.

Much has to be done to more fully meet the demand for manufactured goods and services, saturate the home market with needed items, improve quality and offer a wide assortment of goods, make the price system more flexible and raise the standard of trade. A comprehensive program of promoting consumer goods production and developing public services has been worked out for the purpose of fulfilling these tasks. The program provides for a considerable increase in the output of quality clothes and footwear and modern household goods and durables and for a further development of various services.

This program will be approved in the near future. Meanwhile, as you know, the Central Committee and the USSR Council of Ministers have already adopted resolutions on some of its aspects, such as the increase in the production of footwear, the development of local industries, house-building and repair services, improvement of telephone communication services for the population, and so on. It is important that the Soviet people should feel a change for the better as soon as possible.

We must take into account the changes that are taking place in the structure of the solvent demand. Working people want to spend a greater part of their incomes on improving housing and amenities, on leisure activities, on tours and excursions, etc. These requirements must be met more fully. It is profitable for the state, too. But the possibilities are not being adequately used. Let us take, for example, such a specific question as the development of market-gardening and vegetable-growing cooperatives. This is a very useful undertaking which interests many people. However, it has not yet received all the attention it deserves. The demand for plots of land and cottages, building materials and tools is far from being satisfied. The Politburo has discussed the question in great detail and has instructed the relevant agencies to take appropriate measures so that people's demands can be met as fully as possible and all unreasonable barriers be removed.

Public health and education are the two spheres that are becoming ever more important in the life of our society and every individual, and consequently in the Party's social policy. We have achieved a good deal in their development, making these vitally important benefits equally accessible to all citizens.

Nevertheless, today we are facing new tasks in this respect.

From the point of view of modern requirements, there should be a considerable improvement of the material and technical basis of the public health system and the quality of medical services. The population should be better supplied with medicines. Not long ago the Politburo discussed the need for large-scale measures in this sphere, which should be provided for the Twelfth five-year period development plans.

We have launched school reform, the significance of which for the country's future can hardly be overestimated. Even now set tasks should be approached in a meaningful rather than a formal way, and the quality of teaching and upbringing of the younger generations—as well as preparing them for socially useful labor—should be basically improved.

There are quite a few other problems to which we should pay close attention and find the right solutions. These are an improvement of living standards for labor veterans, especially those who retired a long time ago, an improvement of the living conditions of young families, and an improvement of mother-and-child care. And naturally, it is important to continue to step up efforts aimed at solving such a socially important problem as housing so that every family will soon be provided with a separate flat or house with all the amenities.

As much attention as possible must be given to everything concerning people, their work, material welfare and leisure. For us, this is the focal point of all policy making.

Let us now turn to the problems at hand, i.e. those involved in the implementation of this year's plan. We did not begin the year too well. In the first quarter, the increase in industrial output amounted to a mere two per cent. The greatest lag could be seen in oil, metal and power production, as well as transport. The rates of growth in labor productivity have slowed down. The situation with production costs, profit and other indicators is not much better. In April, the situation was levelling out a bit, but it will take a much greater effort in the remaining eight months to catch up on what has been missed. We must be frank and say that this is no easy task, but the 1985 plan has to be fulfilled, and this must be done without introducing any corrections to the plan. Socialist emulation as well as all organizational and political work must be directed toward this aim.

Farmers are facing responsible tasks, too. High results, pleasing to the entire country, are expected from them.

At the same time, we must see to it that the plan for the next year and the Twelfth five-year plan period as a whole is thoroughly worked out. To achieve this, it would seem advisable to make the plan targets and norms known to ministries, departments, industrial amalgamations and enterprises as soon as possible. This would enable the work collectives' proposals on mobilizing reserves to be taken into account as much as possible, and, what is particularly important, to start the Twelfth five-year plan period in a well-organized and energetic manner from the very first day of the next year.

Comrades, the complex and large-scale tasks of the present period, which involve every aspect of our life, can only be solved if we rely on the creative endeavor, talent, wisdom and work of all the people. We must instill in millions of workers the desire to fulfill these tasks. We must steadily promote the initiative and energy of the working class, collective farmers and intelligentsia. We must set in motion the inexhaustible reserves of socialist society and more actively support all useful undertakings.

The Leninist Party, the Party of Communists, has always been and continues to be in the forefront. Today the Party is expected to lead in the nationwide drive to intensify the country's social and economic development. To this end, every Party organization and every Communist must join in the struggle for accomplishing both short-term and long-term tasks.

Preparations for the Congress, the forthcoming reports and elections, must enhance in a comprehensive way the upsurge in Communists' activity and responsibility, the strengthening of the efficiency of the Party organizations, the consolidation of their ties with the masses and, in the long run, the enhancing of the Party's leading role.

The report to the constituency and election campaign will start with the primary organizations, which are the Party's main dynamo. It is in them that the Party policy is being translated into real work. It is in them that our successes and shortcomings, our possibilities and reserves are particularly evident.

That is why it is so important that when Communists hold meetings the results of what has already been done should be summed up in a Leninist way, without false idealization or idle talk, that all the positive experience should be gleaned carefully, that shortcomings should be exposed fearlessly, and the possibilities and specific ways of achieving the growth of production, of raising the economy's effectiveness and of improving work should be discovered.

The duty of the Party committees is to show the utmost concern that the meetings of the primary organizations are held in a businesslike manner, in an atmosphere of criticism and self-criticism, of Bolshevist frankness, and that the most urgent questions concerning the life of work collectives and the ways of removing everything that slows work down are discussed. It is essential to make sure that each Party member is fully able to use his right, provided by the Party Rules, to make proposals and comments so that not a single critical remark is ignored.

The question of strengthening order and discipline is particularly relevant today. It is an imperative demand of the day. The Soviet people see it as including order in production and in the service industries, in public and daily life, in every working unit, in every town and village. And we shall spare no effort in making sure that such order is strengthened in the country.

Life has shown how the measures for establishing order meet with the unanimous support of the people and what tangible results they produce. But it must be said frankly that attention to this most important question has been rather lax in recent times. And in this case we must, above all, make the managers of collectives who bear personal responsibility for discipline more strictly responsible. It is not entirely uncommon to come across the instances when managers of enterprises forgive the lack of discipline among their workers in the hope that their subordinates will, in their turn, pardon their own mistakes. We shall not be reconciled to such a psychology of mutual forgiveness.

One other condition must be met if discipline and order are to be strengthened. Each one has to do his own work and to carry out his direct responsibilities honestly. It is impossible to achieve substantial results in any field before a Party functionary stops replacing a manager, an engineer a messenger, and a researcher stops working at a vegetable depot and a weaver on a farm. Unfortunately, that is often the case today. Of course, such a situation has not arisen overnight and is determined by certain difficulties in some places. Neither can it be rectified overnight. But it must be rectified. Only then will we be genuinely able to rid ourselves of irresponsibility and laxity.

Greater demands should be put on the tone, businesslike manner and exactingness at the forthcoming district, city, regional and territorial Party conferences and the Congresses of the Communist Parties of the Union Republics. There should be no expressions of praise and compliments, as is sometimes the case, and no attempts should be made to conceal the essence of the matter behind general verbiage, or to explain away shortcomings by referring to objective circumstances or departmental discrepancies.

We expect the leading personnel, the Central Committee members, the heads of ministries and departments to take a direct part not only in the Party conferences but also in the meetings of primary organizations and do everything for the pre-Congress collective council of the Communists to be held in the most constructive way and in the spirit of utmost criticism.

The main slogans of the moment, which must be the keynote of our pre-Congress meetings and all the preparations for the Twenty-seventh Party Congress, are creative endeavor, the unity between words and deeds, initiative and responsibility, exactingness toward oneself and one's comrades. Communists must set an example. It is necessary to increase the responsibility of each Party member for his attitude to his public duty, for the fulfillment of Party decisions, for the honest and pure image of a Party member. A Communist is assessed by what he does. There are no, nor can there be, any other criteria.

The leading Party bodies are to be formed in the course of

the reports and elections. They must be supplemented by fresh forces and the urgent questions regarding personnel should be resolved. The recent plenary meetings held by Party committees have demonstrated convincingly what mature personnel the Party has at its disposal. At the same time, they have confirmed once again the need for abiding, in the strictest manner, by the Leninist principles of selecting, distributing and educating personnel. In those places where these principles are violated, where the promotion of workers is allowed on the basis of personal loyalty, servility and protectionism, criticism and self-criticism inevitably falter, the ties with the masses are weakened and as a result failures in the work occur.

The Politburo regards it as fundamentally important to continue upholding the course of securing the stability of Party leadership and the correct combination of experienced and young workers. But this cannot be accompanied by any kind of stagnation in the movement of personnel. In their letters to the Central Committee, Communists draw attention to the fact that some leaders occupying one and the same post for a long time quite often stop seeing what is new and get used to shortcomings. This gives food for thought and calls for a search for ways to ensure more active promotion of our leading personnel. Women and promising young workers should be promoted to responsible posts more boldly.

And one more important conclusion which has been prompted by the recent plenary meetings of Party committees. Not a single Party organization, not a single worker, can remain outside regulation. The first secretaries of the Central Committees of the Communist Parties of many Union Republics, and territorial and regional Party committees have reported in the last two years to the meetings of the Politburo and the Secretariat of the CPSU Central Committee. Reports were heard from the leaders of a number of primary Party organizations, district and city Party committees, and of many ministries and departments. This kind of work must, of course, be done in the future as well and be actively developed in the Republics, territories and regions. This is in agreement with the norms of our inner-

Party life.

Since we have started speaking about regulation, I would like to make the following observation. It is necessary to check up and to regulate, and each checkup should be of practical use and serve the interests of the cause. But checkups on one and the same quite often insignificant question and numerous commissions which are set up out of formal considerations, distracting people from their work and creating a tense atmosphere, are hardly justified.

Reporting sessions with constituency, conferences and congresses provide an opportunity for comprehensively evaluating the activities of the elected Party bodies and for making a close study of the content and methods of their work. Emphasis should be placed, first of all, on analyzing their ability to cope with the key questions concerning people's life and work production collectives, development of the economy and culture, and on how organizational work is being conducted among the masses. It is necessary to continue persistently to provide daily and concrete assistance to primary Party organizations, to ensure greater efficiency and promptness, to reduce paper flow, to overcome the armchair method of work and the craving for numerous meetings and conferences.

It must be honestly said that far from everything has been done in the struggle against such phenomena. There are quite a few examples of this. Not so long ago the CPSU Central Committee heard the reports from the Kalinin and Tselinograd Regional Party Committees on questions concerning the development of the agroindustrial complex. Serious shortcomings were revealed in the Party's guidance of the economy, in the personnel and educational work and in the activities of the bureaus and the secretaries of the regional committees. The main thing which gave rise to the shortcomings in this case was the uncritical attitude to what had been done, the tendency toward exaggerating the results achieved and the reluctance to notice negative phenomena. The appropriate measures had to be taken as a result.

Some heads of ministries and departments adhere to the old

methods in management and display a lack of self-criticism. This hinders work. Life itself puts on the agenda the need for a decisive improvement of work and for bringing it into conformity with the demands of the present-day stage in society's development.

Today mere diligence is not enough, though even this is lacking sometimes. Competence, the feeling for what is new, initiative, boldness and a readiness to shoulder responsibility, the ability to set a task and see it through, the ability not to lose sight of the political meaning of management—these businesslike qualities are becoming increasingly important. And I would also add the desire to learn how to work.

Further enhancement of the Party guidance of the Soviets, trade unions, Komsomol and other links in our political system and of all the work for the development of Soviet democracy is an important task of reports and the election campaign.

We must always remember Lenin's words that socialist democracy must not be understood in the abstract. It remains, as it has always been, an instrument for the development of the economy, the growth in man's activity and the communist education of the masses. And in this way the Party will work, as before, as it enriches the democratic nature of the Soviet system.

The preparations for the Twenty-seventh Party Congress and the discussion by working people of the drafts of the Congress documents will, of course, enhance the activity of the Soviet people. The Party committees are to ensure publicity, see to it that the channels of communication with the masses are working and that attention is being given to public opinion, critical comments and applications and letters sent by citizens. The CPSU Central Committee regards them as being very helpful, a tangible expression of the interest displayed by the Soviet people in the affairs of their own state.

The Central Committee has often discussed the tasks of the Party's political-educational and ideological work. The attention paid to this work is understandable and some progress has also been made. But, as I see it, far from everything has been done to bring ideological work closer to life. Formalism and exhortations continue to be a hindrance. Quite often the loss comes from idle talk and from the inability to tell people the truth. And it sometimes happens that a person hears one thing but sees something else in real life. This is a serious question and not only an educational one but a political one, too.

Ideological and political education in all its forms must be coupled as much as possible with the main task of our time—the acceleration of the country's socioeconomic development. This cannot be achieved without a comprehensive account being taken of the totality of conditions in our internal life and the specifics of the international situation. You know that it was precisely to these questions that the All-Union Scientific and Practical Conference held last December was devoted. The conference also discussed the fulfillment of the decisions of the June 1983 Plenary Meeting of the CPSU Central Committee. It would be appropriate to point out today once more that there must be—let it not seem a paradox to anyone—less words and more deeds in propaganda and in ideological work as a whole, too.

Special mention should be made of the work done by the mass media—from the factory and local media to the central media. The press, TV and radio are an effective means for organizing and educating the masses and for shaping public opinion. Positive changes have been taking place in their work recently. But life demands more.

The media are called upon to make a profound analysis of events and phenomena, to raise important questions and propose the ways for solving them, to be convincing in their content, prompt reportage and abundance of information. An intelligent word from the Party addressed to the individual gives food for thought, arouses people's initiative and fosters in them an irreconcilable attitude to shortcomings. The effectiveness of the press, TV and radio increases considerably when the Party committees give them their active support and assistance. It is only necessary that this assistance and support should always be timely and significant. And, of course, any attempts to suppress or ignore well-founded criticisms should get a principled Party assessment.

Literature and the arts play a great role in enriching society's intellectual life with new values and in the ideological and moral development of the Soviet people. The artistic intelligentsia—writers, poets, composers, artists and theater and cinema workers—enjoy great prestige and recognition. But this also makes them greatly responsible to society. All of the best which has been created by Soviet literature and the arts has been always inseparable from the main activities and concerns of the Party and the people. There is no doubt that the new tasks which are being tackled today will find a befitting response in the creative endeavor which affirms the truth of socialist life.

These, Comrades, are our tasks and the main trends in our domestic and foreign policies. They will of course be discussed in detail at this Plenary Meeting which is to determine the nature of the pre-Congress work of the entire Party and of each of its organizations.

We must hold the Plenary Meeting in a way which would allow us to sum it up in Lenin's own words:

"We know our tasks today much more clearly, concretely and thoroughly than we did yesterday. We are not afraid of pointing openly to our mistakes in order to rectify them. We shall now devote all the Party's efforts to improving its organization, to enriching the quality and content of its work, to creating closer contact with the masses, and to working out increasingly correct and accurate working-class tactics and strategy."

The Party and the Soviet people expect from us comprehensive, well-thought-out and responsible decisions and it can be said in all confidence that they will be supported by the Communists and by all the people. This support will find its expression in their social awareness, their activity and their work.

April 23, 1985

22

THE KEY ISSUE
OF THE PARTY'S
ECONOMIC POLICY

AS YOU KNOW, Comrades, the decisions of the April Plenary Meeting of the Central Committee have been received with wide approval by Communists and the entire Soviet people. This is clear from the results of work of the plenary meetings of the Party committees and the numerous comments sent to the central bodies. Everywhere working people are showing increased concern for the affairs of state and society. They express a wish to move forward, to wage more actively the campaign for strengthening order in all spheres of our life, to be firm and consistent in this effort. In a word, a good, businesslike atmosphere is emerging in Party organizations, work collectives and the country as a whole.

Relying on the experience of building socialism, the achievements of the Soviet economy and the scientific elaboration of the CPSU's long-term strategy, the April Plenary Meeting formulated the concept of accelerating the country's socioeconomic development on the basis of scientific and technological progress.

The decision of the Politburo of the Central Committee to hold this meeting before the Twenty-seventh Congress of the CPSU is motivated by the need for urgent measures in that field.

In advancing the task of accelerating socioeconomic development, the Central Committee has in mind not just an increase in economic growth rates. The point at issue is a new quality as regards our development, rapid progress in the strategically important fields, a structural rebuilding of production, a transfer to intensive methods and effective forms of management and a more comprehensive solution of social problems.

The need to accelerate socioeconomic development is determined by our internal requirements. We have much to be proud of in the development of our economy. Thousands of plants have been built in this country, the face of our cities and villages has changed, and standards of culture, education and health care have improved. Much has been done to improve the housing, cultural and everyday living conditions and material well-being of the people in general. This is another clear manifestation of the advantages of socialism, of a planned economy. Our successes are indisputable. They have been generally recognized.

Yet one cannot help noting that from the early 1970s certain difficulties began to be felt in economic development. The main reason is that we did not show in good time perseverance in reshaping structural policy, forms and methods of management and the very psychology of economic activity.

The Party and the whole people are faced with the task of overcoming negative trends and bringing about a sharp turn for the better. Any other approach is out of the question. We cannot embark on curtailing social programs. Confronting society are the urgent problems of improving food supply and increasing the output of goods and services for the people. It is important to continue housing construction on a large scale, improve medical services and develop education, science and culture.

At the same time, Mikhail Gorbachev pointed out, the need to accelerate socioeconomic development arises from external factors. We are forced to invest the necessary funds in the country's defense. The Soviet Union will continue to make every effort to put an end to the arms race, but in the face of imperialism's aggressive policy and threats we must not permit military superiority over us. Such is the will of the Soviet people.

In the eyes of the world's progressive public, the Soviet Union has been and remains an embodiment of the age-old social aspirations of people. It must also set an example by achieving high organizational standards and economic efficiency. Therefore, the task of accelerating the country's development has today assumed paramount political, economic and social significance. Implementation of this task is an urgent matter for the whole Party and nation.

As the Party prepares for its Twenty-seventh Congress and as the program documents of that congress are being drawn up, it is vital that we should realize that we cannot do without accelerating scientific and technological progress. Therefore, all of those documents, above all the Guidelines for the country's economic and social development for the period of the Twelfth five-year plan and up to the year 2000, must define new approaches that would ensure a sharp turn toward intensification of the economy.

The Politburo of the Central Committee has recently discussed the draft of the Guidelines and has on the whole approved the target figures and objectives outlined in it. But serious criticism was also voiced, which means that more work on the draft is needed. The draft does not yet include measures that would enable a number of industries to go over to predominantly intensive development; nor are all indicators balanced. Work on the draft must continue, and the objectives for increased production efficiency should be regarded as the minimum.

The main thing now is to identify and put to use all reserves for raising production efficiency and improving output quality. Our cadres should understand the vital need for reorienting every plant, sector, the whole national economy toward an intensive path of development.

Many heads of ministries wish to "wrest" as much capital investment and resources as possible, while being assigned the smallest plans possible. Enviable persistence in trying to get additional funds and have plan target figures reduced is shown by Konstantin N. Belyak, Minister of Mechanical Engineering for Livestock Farming and Fodder Production. A no more commendable stand has been taken by the USSR Ministry of the Building Materials Industry headed by Alexei I. Yashin, and some other ministries and departments. I believe that we are not traveling along the same way as those executives who want to draw the country again into vast, unjustified spending.

In the effort to ensure the effectiveness of investment great exactingness must be displayed toward local executives as well. Major decisions have been taken on the development of the productive forces of the Krasnoyarsk Territory on the initiative of the territorial Party committee and with the support of several ministries and the USSR State Planning Committee. The

Krasnoyarsk Territory is a big and promising region, which should be developed in every way possible. But work should be done there, as everywhere, with an eye to speedy repayment of the money invested. Regrettably, this has not happened. The Sayano-Shushenskoye hydropower station is being built at a rate only half as fast as the Bratsk station. For several years now the buildings of the Abakan railway carriage factory have been standing empty. Five thousand projects are yet to be completed in the Territory. As a result of the scattering of resources, construction is proceeding slowly and resource losses are great. Are not the Party organization of the Territory, its planning and economic bodies responsible for this? The state will continue to provide unstintingly for the development of Siberia. But we have the right to demand that resources should be used to full effect.

Now, at the stage of drafting the Twelfth Five-Year Plan, an example of thrift in economic management must be shown by the leading industrial regions. The Central Committee places great hopes on Moscow's working class and intelligentsia and on the capital's powerful scientific and industrial potential. We would like to express our support once again for the important work being done by the Leningrad Party organization. Interesting proposals have been worked out by Communists of the Chelyabinsk Region. We also have a right to expect a greater contribution to accelerating scientific and technological progress from such industrial centers as Sverdlovsk and Kharkov, Novosibirsk and Donetsk, Omsk and others. The Central Committee hopes that their Party organizations will see to it that measures to put the economy on the road of intensive development are carried out.

All this is being said so that now, in the time that is left for the work on the Guidelines and the drafting of the five-year plan, an approach that would not only ensure attainment of the targets outlined in the draft but also their overfulfillment should be taken at all levels. We must attain even higher targets with less expenditure. Such is the economic and, if you like, political task.

Then Mikhail Gorbachev dwelt in detail on problems of

changing investment and structural policy. The main emphasis should be put on the technical re-equipment of enterprises, the economizing of resources and the ensuring of a marked improvement in the quality of products.

It is crucial to discard without a moment's hesitation the economic management stereotype of the past, under which new construction was considered the main way of expanding production, while many operating enterprises were not modernized for many years. As people say, everything possible was squeezed out, but very little was put in.

Today a considerable part of the production assets have become obsolete, as a result of which the volume of capital repair work has increased excessively. Returns on assets are falling and the number of new workplaces is growing, while at the same time mechanization is being introduced on an insufficient scale. The share of manual labor is decreasing rather slowly.

No one disputes today that capital investment in modernization yields a return approximately twice as great as that in new construction. But the previous, extensive methods of economic management are unfortunately very tenacious. Fifty billion roubles of capital investment have been earmarked, for instance, for the iron and steel industry over a period of fifteen years. Most of it was channeled into new, non-integrated construction projects, but no attention was given to the technical re-equipment of enterprises. Because of the wrong technical policy of the Board of the Iron and Steel Ministry and of Minister Ivan P. Kazanets, this industry has failed to fulfill the assignments of both the Tenth and the Eleventh five-year plans. The state of affairs here calls for cardinal changes.

On a countrywide scale, the share of funds channeled into modernization in the total volume of capital investment should be raised from one third to at least one half within the next few years. This is not a simple matter. We cannot do without new construction. But projects under construction should be given serious attention. Some of them should be speeded up and others suspended or even mothballed.

At the same time a general stocktaking of production assets should be carried out and a program drawn up for the re-equipment of every enterprise, and every industry. The share of outdated fixed assets to be withdrawn, especially of their active part, should be doubled. And what is needed is not just any renewal of production but the kind that involves introduction of the most advanced technology and brings the greatest economic and social results.

The ratio between capital investments in industries that extract, process and consume resources presents a big and pressing problem. It is becoming ever more difficult to increase the output of fuel and raw materials. But there is a more rational way, that of all-round economy and wide introduction of resource-saving technologies. This cuts costs two to three times. The Ministry of Electrical Engineering, for instance, has gained good experience in resource saving. As a result, the growth of output in this industry in the Eleventh five-year plan period is being achieved without increasing consumption of basic materials.

On the whole, our economy remains in many respects an extravagant one. Up to eight million tons of gasoline are unnecessarily burned up every year owing to the lag in re-equipping the fleet of motor vehicles with diesel engines. Because of inefficient equipment at thermal power stations, we annually overspend more than twenty million tons of standard fuel. There are hundreds of thousands of primitive boiler rooms in this country which use fuel irrationally. Resources that can be recycled are not being used effectively. Meanwhile, resource saving should be one of the main aims of investment policy. The task is to meet seventy-five to eighty per cent of the increase in the requirements of the national economy in fuel, raw materials and other materials through saving.

Careful consideration, consistency and the need for quick economic results are very important in investment policy. Of course, a certain order of priorities is inevitable in carrying out any measures. But once we have set ourselves tasks, they must be carried out fully, comprehensively, quickly and energetically.

We must not allow capital investments to be allotted without regard to who needs them most. In the new five-year plan period we must concentrate capital investments more resolutely on the most economically effective sectors. This refers, for instance, to the agroindustrial complex, where the level of capital investments has reached optimum dimensions while the returns on them are as yet insufficient.

Mechanical engineering plays the main, key role in the scientific and technological revolution. Already in the Twelfth five-year plan period its growth rate should be raised by fifty to one hundred per cent. The task is to make maximum use of available capacities and to modernize this industry as a matter of top priority. For this purpose capital investment in mechanical engineering should be increased, through partial re-distribution, by eighty to one hundred per cent and the volume of supply of modern types of equipment sharply raised.

A task of special importance is organizing mass production of equipment of new generations, capable of assuring a manifold increase in labor productivity and opening the way to the automation of all stages of the production process. It is important to go over to the supply of complete sets of equipment and to have large-scale repair and maintenance services provided by manufacturers.

Microelectronics, computer technology and instrument making, indeed the entire information science industry is a catalyst of technological progress. This needs to be developed at an accelerated pace. No doubt a great deal depends not only on increasing the output of computers but on their competent use in the national economy. We have taken major decisions on this matter and their fulfillment must be strictly monitored.

In short, boosting Soviet mechanical engineering is the main road of our development, a road that should be unswervingly followed, now and in the future.

The state of affairs in capital construction should also be assessed from the point of view of accelerating scientific and technological progress. This problem has been on the agenda for many years, but so far there has been no major improvement here. This reduces to naught in many ways our efforts in the sphere of scientific and technological advance.

There are often ineffective technological solutions in the project designs themselves. Consequently quite a few of them have to be returned each year for revision. Fragmentation of capital investment continues and the time limits of construction work are incredibly prolonged. As a result, even the finest projects become hopelessly outdated. We cannot carry on construction work this way any longer. Things should be put in better order in construction planning and design to ensure concentration of capital investment, observance of time limits for the completion of construction projects and to make construction work a single industrial process.

The efficiency of the national economy and its growth rates depends in many ways on the structure and quality of materials. In this matter we are as yet behind modern requirements. It is known, for instance, that we produce more steel than any other country and yet we are chronically short of metal. The main reasons for this lie in poor quality of metal, a limited range of metal products and wasteful use of metal. The share of plastics, ceramics and other advanced non-metallic materials in the overall volume of materials has been small so far. In the world today there is a real boom of small-volume chemical production and of the production of pure and super-pure materials which determine in many respects the level of present-day technology. Therefore we need to double or treble our efforts in order not to fall behind.

The problems of the production infrastructure have become more acute at the present stage of economic development. The backlog in transport, communications, material and technical supplies and other sectors leads to great losses. We must seek additional means of solving this acute economic problem.

The tasks of accelerating scientific and technological progress, the speaker went on, require that we should take a new approach to all our external economic activities. The country's foreign trade turnover has reached 140 billion roubles. But the rates of its growth can and must be increased and, what is most important, the pattern of our exports and imports must be improved.

Our machinery and equipment exports have been growing slowly in recent years. There are several reasons for this: The low competitiveness of many of them and insufficient interest on the part of industrial enterprises in producing export goods. We must not put up with this any longer. In import policy we should use more effectively the opportunities offered by a mutually beneficial international division of labor. This refers, of course, first of all, to our relations with CMEA countries. The speaker raised as a matter of urgency the question of the need for more efficient use of imported equipment. As an example of a careless attitude to it, mention was made of the work of the Ministry of the Oil-Processing and Petrochemical Industry of the USSR. Minister Viktor S. Fyodorov had given assurances more than once that he would rectify the shortcomings. But evidently he is not keeping his promises. The CPSU Central Committee has given instructions that the matter be thoroughly looked into and the results of the inquiry reported to the Politburo.

The new technical re-equipment of the national economy will require enormous capital investments.

Where are we to find them? The main answer to this question is that measures designed to speed up scientific and technological progress should pay for themselves. Indeed, they are being carried out for the purpose of raising labor productivity and therefore of speeding up growth in national income. But this will take some time, while the funds are needed immediately. So we cannot do here without maneuvering resources, concentrating them on the key areas.

A top-priority task is to mobilize organizational, economic and social factors, to put things in order everywhere and to improve the organization of production so as to ensure the most efficient utilization of what the country has. Each amalgamation and enterprise, each production unit should identify the sections where maximum effect can be obtained at minimum outlay, and perhaps without any outlay at all. It should be firmly established in everyone's mind that a regime of economy is the road to our prosperity and is indeed the task of all tasks. It is a task for the whole Party, the entire nation.

A certain shift toward improvement in output quality, which is the most precise and comprehensive indicator of scientific and technological progress, of work efficiency and discipline has taken place in recent years. But we must recognize that the quality, the technical and economic standard of products remains a vulnerable element in our economy, a source of many difficulties and problems. All this does serious social, economic, moral and political damage. And it is totally unacceptable when newly-made equipment turns out to be outdated even at the design stage and is below the best standards as regards reliability, service life and efficiency. By their parameters even products considered to be of the highest category sometimes do not bear comparison with the best world models. There must be stricter observance of the requirements that are to be met when the state quality mark is awarded to a product. Output quality should be a matter not just of professional, but also of national pride.

The problem of quality, of course, cannot be solved at one stroke. But in this work there can be no justification for any procrastination whatsoever. Nobody has the right to remain on the sidelines here—not a single enterprise, not a single designer, production engineer or scientist, not a single worker or collective farmer, in short, not a single honest salary or wage earner. The Party will actively support the campaign for enhancing the prestige of the Soviet trademark and will strictly call to account those who take a passive stand, who hamper the solution of this very acute problem.

The front line of struggle to accelerate scientific and technological progress is in the scientific area. The successes of Soviet scientists in various fields of knowledge and technological progress are universally acknowledged. We can be proud of our achievements in space research, mathematics and mechanics, thermonuclear synthesis, quantum electronics and several areas in biology. Promising work is being done in almost every sphere of science and technology.

At the same time we must look at the tasks facing science through the prism of present-day requirements, and that means that science should make a resolute turn toward the needs of social production, while production should turn toward science. It is from this point of view that we must analyze and consolidate all the links in the chain combining science, technology and production.

The development of fundamental science should be given foremost importance. It is fundamental science that is the generator of ideas, making breakthroughs possible into new fields and showing ways of attaining new levels of efficiency. Here we must enhance the role of the USSR Academy of Sciences. We must bring about a sharp turn in the work of the Academy's institutes toward expanding research of a technical nature, increasing their role in and responsibility for the formulation of the theoretical principles of fundamentally new types of machinery and technology. The scientific potential of universities and institutes is an important reserve, and we are still not making full use of the possibilities it affords. According to existing estimates, establishments of higher education can increase the volume of research by 100-150 per cent.

Greater demands should be made of the research establishments under the various ministries, and their performance deserves serious criticism. Hundreds of research establishments, development and design organizations are subordinated to the industrial ministries. Many of them are isolated from production and are not geared to achieving high economic results. The Ministry of the Chemical Industry, for instance, is literally overgrown with a multitude of various scientific establishments and experimental production facilities. But it is in that industry that major shortcomings have been uncovered in the development of new materials and techniques. We can cite concrete examples of inefficiency in some of the ministerial research institutes.

We must perfect organizational and economic forms of integration of science, technology and production. For example, the creation of integrated intersectoral scientific-technical centers within the framework of the USSR Academy of Sciences has proven very effective, judging by the experience of the Paton Institute of Electric Welding and other scientific institutions.

In order to overcome the problem of isolation of institutes and development and design organizations from production many of them should now be made parts of amalgamations and enterprises, thus strengthening research potential at the factory level. It is very important to impart a new impulse to all work involved in the expansion of the network of large research-and-production amalgamations, which should in turn become genuine outposts of scientific and technological progress, as "Kriogenmash," "Svetlana" and many other amalgamations have already done.

While giving prime attention to bolstering large research and technical organizations, we must simultaneously actively support the work of inventors and innovators, find means of selecting significant technical proposals and ensure their more prompt application in industry.

A great deal will have to be accomplished in order that research and technical development might quickly yield considerable economic results. The CPSU Central Committee and the Soviet Government count on the country's scientists and the entire scientific-technical intelligentsia to take close to heart the tasks set forth by the Party and to spare no effort in accelerating scientific and technological progress.

Life calls for a thorough restructuring of the planning and management of the entire economic mechanism. In principle the main direction of the restructuring of economic management is clear to us. It is the ensurance of deeper and more widespread utilization of the advantages of a socialist economy. We must advance along a line toward further consolidation and development of democratic centralism. The primary essence of the restructuring is to increase the efficiency of centralism in management and planning, to expand the independence and responsibility of enterprises, to make active use of the more flexible forms and methods of management, cost accounting, and commodity-monetary relations and to extensively develop the initiative of the masses.

The economy should be made maximally responsive to scientific and technological progress, and we must ensure that all sectors of the economy have a vital stake in this. Party and economic bodies are working vigorously to resolve these problems. New branches are constantly being included in the large-scale economic experiment. However, it is necessary to make a transition from experiment to the creation of an integral management and control system.

We must start from the upper echelons. Lenin's idea of turning the State Planning Committee into a scientific-economic body employing prominent scientists and leading specialists must be practically implemented. A primary position in the plans should be given to qualitative indicators showing the effectiveness of the use of resources, the scale of modernization of output and growth of labor productivity on the basis of scientific and technological progress.

The CPSU Central Committee is receiving numerous proposals on the place and role of the State Committee for Science and Technology. The idea is that the committee be made responsible for exercising control over the scientific and technical standard of the economic sectors, the extent of correspondence of production to the best achievements, the formation of the country's network of research institutions and design organizations and for the coordination of scientific and technical activities.

The principal reserves for the attainment of greatest effectiveness lie in those areas where the sectors overlap. It is illusory to hope that the State Planning Committee will be able to look into all the links of the chain of intersectoral connections and choose the optimum variant. Nor can the ministries cope with this job. All this places on the order of the day the question of creating management bodies for large economic complexes. The role and functions of the ministries under the new conditions will have to change. They will be able to concentrate maximum attention on long-term planning and large-scale use of innovations for raising the technical standard of production and products. There must be considerable reduction in administrative staff in the economic sectors, with unnecessary sectors being cut.

A great deal must be done to perfect the structure of the republic management bodies, where the number of ministries and departments is far too great and continues to grow. There the problem of integration and concentration of management is even more poignant than on the national level.

The role of the main production link—amalgamations and enterprises—must be enhanced to accelerate scientific and technological progress. The center of gravity of all day-to-day economic work must be shifted here, and they must be subordinated, as a rule, directly to the ministries. The necessary work does not consist of "patching up holes," merging or splitting organizations, or moving executives from one office to another. We must resolve matters pertaining to streamlining the organizational structure boldly, with good substantiation and, most importantly, in a not less than comprehensive manner, from the upper to the lower echelons, both vertically and horizontally.

Restructuring of the organizational pattern of management should be organically tied to the reinforcement of cost accounting, economic levers and incentives. We need a mechanism actually guaranteeing advantages to work collectives which are successful in accelerating scientific and technological progress. We need a mechanism making the output of outdated and ineffective products unprofitable. To this end we must first of all take steps to increase the consumer's influence on the technical level and quality of products. Price formation should be radically improved to facilitate successful realization of the economic policy and rapid implementation of everything new and advanced.

Amalgamations and enterprises must be completely transferred to a self-supporting system, with the number of centrally-issued plan assignments sharply reduced. It has been known to happen, and not infrequently, that ministries and even All-Union production amalgamations arbitrarily include many unnecessary indices in their plans. It is time we established legislative order here. The activities of enterprises should be regulated to an ever greater extent by economic norms.

Amalgamations and enterprises should be given an opportunity to earn for themselves the means necessary for raising the technical level of production and the quality of products, for social development, and for using these funds at their own discretion, drawing widely on the credits. It is very important to establish a close interdependence between workers' performance and their pay. The two must be directly connected. It is important to more boldly extend the principles of the collective contract to the work of amalgamations and enterprises, and actively set up enlarged integrated teams working on a cost-accounting basis.

We must eliminate everything outdated so that a "cost-conscious economic machinery," if I may put it that way, can operate unimpeded and literally slap the hands of inefficient executives and those anxious to secure maximum resources and capital investment from the state while giving as little as possible back to society.

In short, there is some very serious work ahead needed to improve the system of economic management. This work cannot be put off because we cannot accelerate scientific and technological progress in a real way without creating new economic and organizational conditions.

This task, one of great magnitude, creates the need for far-reaching changes in Party work. This work has to do with the human factor, the decisive factor in all transformations. Hence the main task of this work today is to inspire, by all possible means, a change in the minds and moods of personnel from top to bottom by concentrating their attention on the most important thing—scientific and technological progress. Exactingness and again exactingness is the main thing dictated to us Communists by the present situation. Life's test, a most severe and uncompromising one, is what the Party and all the cadres are undergoing today.

We are discussing a long-term political line, and none of the problems can be put off till tomorrow—they must be solved today. The demands made on our economic, managerial cadres should be raised. There must be no waiting or delay. There is no time left for warming up—it was exhausted in the past. We must move only forward at an ever-increasing speed.

Acceleration of scientific and technological progress calls for a cardinal change in the situation involving engineering, technical and scientific personnel. We must develop measures to secure greater public recognition of the work of scientists and engineers, to strengthen creative principles in it, to stimulate high-quality performance with less manpower, and on this basis to raise their pay. We must increase the Party's influence on the whole course of scientific and technological advancement and strengthen the Party strata in the decisive sectors. Systematic work for the training and retraining of personnel, above all in the new professions resulting from progress in technology, is becoming particularly necessary.

The sources of many shortcomings and miscalculations lie in the fact that the Party committees of the ministries have in some areas dulled their political keenness in perceiving and resolving the most important socioeconomic issues, and have withdrawn from control, the right to which they are accorded by the Rules of the CPSU. Such an approach does not meet the present-day requirements of the country's socio-economic development.

A vast field of activities—definite and responsible—is also opening in ideological and propaganda work. People should be aided in understanding that the acceleration of scientific and technological progress is a vital cause serving the interests of all and enabling all to display their abilities and talent. We count on the creative vigor and skill of our working class, peasantry and intelligentsia, our engineers and scientists. We expect in particular a great deal from young people with their energy and searching minds and their interest in all that is new and progressive.

Let us proceed to touch upon current issues of economic activity. The working people of the country are faced with the important task of successfully completing the current year and the five-year plan period as a whole. It is important for the Party organizations to ensure an overall increase in the production of fuel and other raw materials for industry, to organize timely and high-quality agricultural work, and to harvest and preserve the entire crop. The point is that the country must enter the new five-year plan period with good performance behind it and in an organized manner.

In conclusion Mikhail Gorbachev said:

The business at hand is formidable. It is innovative, difficult, and of great magnitude. Will we be able to cope with it? The Central Committee is confident that we will. We are obliged to do so. But this will require of each of us intensive thought, determined work, enormous concentration, consciousness and organization. It is not in the Party's traditions, nor in the character of the Soviet people to fear tasks because of their complexity, to retreat before difficulties or to slacken up and indulge in self-complacency, especially at turning points, at responsible moments in the country's life.

When the Soviet Republic was making the first steps toward socialism in an extremely difficult situation, Lenin wrote with confidence:

"We will extricate ourselves because we do not try to make our position look better than it is. We realize all the difficulties. We see *all* the maladies, and are taking measures to cure them methodically, with perseverance, and without giving way to panic."

Today too, profound faith in the creative energy of the workers, peasants and intellectuals, and in the high moral spirit and determination of the people nourishes the Party's optimism. But optimism does not free anybody of the need to work. We will have to work hard. The CPSU's policy enjoys the support of the whole of society. Soviet people lay great hopes in the ideas, initiatives and plans with which the Party is approaching its Twenty-seventh Congress.

It is the duty of the Party of Communists to justify these hopes, to show that we are tackling the job earnestly. Relying on the people's creative endeavor and cementing the alliance of science and labor, we will have enough energy and fortitude to ensure that our words are matched by deeds. And this is the principal thing in politics, in life.

June 11, 1985

23

ACCELERATING
THE DEVELOPMENT
OF SIBERIA

This speech was made at the Conference of Party and Managerial Activists of the Tyumen and Tomsk Regions (Western Siberia).

ON BEHALF of the Central Committee of the Party, Mikhail Gorbachev warmly and cordially greeted the oil and gas workers, geologists, builders, transport and power workers, scientists—all those who have by their selfless labor, will and energy breathed life into what were once the remotest of areas and created the country's major fuel and energy base there.

To the Soviet people, he said, Tyumen has come to epitomize the outstanding labor effort of hundreds of thousands of workers and specialists. Oil and gas, extracted from the Tyumen region, supply the Soviet Union's farthermost corners from thousands of kilometers away and become a dependable source of the country's further economic development and growing defense capability.

The Soviet people and the Party take pride in your patriotic effort, comrade Siberians!

The oil and gas industry forms the basis of our economy, while the West Siberian complex is its core. The success of our entire national economy largely depends on how well the project operates. For this reason its development is regarded as a matter of paramount importance in the Party's economic strategy.

The Central Committee places much significance on today's conference, its results, and the practical measures that will make for the further advance of the oil and gas industry and for the upsurge in the productive forces of the whole of Siberia.

We hold this meeting at a challenging time for the country. As you are aware, at the April Plenary Meeting of the CPSU Central Committee and at the June Conference of the Central Committee, the Party put forward and substantiated the idea of accelerating Soviet society's social and economic development. Emphasis was placed on scientific and technological progress, on the mobilization of organizational, economic, and social factors, and on thrifty economic management.

Recently, the CPSU Central Committee and the government have adopted important decisions aimed at accelerating the transfer to intensive methods of economic development and raising the efficiency of production. These include comprehensive programs for technologically upgrading mechanical engineering and boosting its development, modernizing the iron and steel industry, perfecting design work and improving all capital construction, introducing fundamentally new technologies, expanding the production and application of computers in the national economy, and so on. Development prospects for the productive forces of some regions of the country have been outlined.

Large-scale measures are being carried out to stimulate scientific and technological progress and accelerate the application of scientific achievements and advanced know-how. Documents have been prepared for a transition to the group management of a number of kindred industries. I think that the decision now being worked out concerning a most important issue—use of manpower resources—will positively effect social and economic life.

Important decisions have also been taken on social matters. I mentioned these earlier.

The CPSU Central Committee understands well that the people have always appraised and will continue to appraise the Party's policy on the basis of deeds performed and results obtained, and not by words or the number of decisions adopted, regardless of how sound they are.

That is why we attach paramount importance to the organization of work to fulfill the decisions adopted, to supervise their implementation. It is precisely this kind of work that must serve as the principal yardstick by which to assess the activities of Party committees and organizations, ministries and departments, government and economic bodies. Any other approach is simply unacceptable. Each person, whatever his job in our society, must be held fully responsible for the work entrusted to him, and he must do it conscientiously and diligently, displaying initiative.

This is of direct concern to you too, dear Comrades. The

Party has called for an accelerated development of our economy. I will tell you straight that to achieve this objective the
country must have the necessary resources of oil and gas. And
that depends on you, first and foremost. Tyumen is the principal
source of hydrocarbon raw materials. We have nothing else like
it. Since the beginning of these fields, the people of Tyumen
have produced over 3 billion tons of oil. The daily output of 1
billion cubic meters of gas, a level achieved sooner than planned,
has been a great success. It is an outstanding achievement,
unsurpassed in the world.

Everything that has been done to build up the oil and gas
industry in Western Siberia is convincing proof of the vast creative potentialities of the socialist system. It is the result of the
outstanding efforts of the 1.5-million-strong multinational
workforce of the Tyumen Region.

It is also clear that such an oil and gas giant as the West
Siberian complex could be built only through the efforts of the
whole country and all its republics. The working people of the
Ukraine, Byelorussia, Uzbekistan, the Baltic and other republics, as well as of Moscow, Leningrad, the autonomous republics,
and territories and regions of the Russian Federation, have made
and continue to make a substantial contribution to its development.

The scale of this work must be expanded. The oilmen of
Tataria and Bashkiria set a good example when they began the
comprehensive development of oilfields in the Tyumen Region.
The proposal of Georgia, Azerbaijan, Moldavia, Armenia and
Turkmenia to have their building organizations participate in
the construction of housing, cultural and social facilities and
establishments, roads, etc., in Western Siberia in the Twelfth
five-year plan period has recently been approved.

Our young people enthusiastically responded to the Party's
call. They have been contributing greatly to the development of
the region's oil and gas reserves. More than 150,000 young
people have come here with Leninist Komsomol assignments.
Student construction teams have done work worth 1.5 billion
roubles. Young people's participation in the development of the

region will continue to grow.

Comrades, a great deal has been done. High targets have been reached. But as time goes on ever new tasks arise. The high targets set in the Energy Program of the USSR and in the Draft Guidelines for the production of oil, and particularly gas, should be met in a great measure through the development of Tyumen deposits.

This is by no means an easy task. It requires the efforts of many people. That is why the Central Committee of the CPSU and the Soviet Government adopted a decision on the comprehensive development of the oil and gas industry of Western Siberia. This fundamental document opens up a qualitatively new stage in the region's development. Its main idea is, in a nutshell, to substantially enhance the efficiency and reliability of the country's fuel production through intensification and the use of the achievements of science and engineering. A major element of this Party document is the measures aimed at improving housing, social and cultural conditions in the life of the oil and gas workers of Siberia and solving a range of social problems in order to expand and consolidate the workforce. A lot of money and resources are allocated for these purposes and they should be used most effectively.

Mikhail Gorbachev stressed that Siberians have to tackle even more complex and important problems. One should always bear in mind, he said, that the success of Tyumen's oil and gas workers strengthen the might of the country and accelerate its advance, and that their failures put the economy into a state of distress and hinder our progress.

For this reason the Party Central Committee is worried by the fact that for three years running the Tyumen Region has been falling short of its oil output targets. This shortfall creates problems in the economy. Moreover, rather than diminishing, the lag is increasing.

Analysis of the situation and the thorough discussion of the urgent problems carried out at this conference have shown that these problems have been accumulating gradually for years. The methods of oil extraction used at the first stage of the development of the oil production center on the Ob River have practically exhausted themselves. It became clear long before today that the time of "fountains of gold," the time of easy oil, so to speak, is coming to an end. Oil is getting harder to extract and we must move to more far-off regions where deposits are not so rich and are more difficult to develop.

We should have studied the problem in depth then, seen the difficulties lying ahead and implemented a program to accommodate a new stage in the development of deposits. But that was not done in time. The central departments as well as Party, government and economic bodies of the Tyumen Region acted too slowly and chose the easiest way to make up for their shortcomings by increasing the load on big deposits. Not only the oilmen but also the building, power engineering and transport workers were not prepared to work under new, complex conditions. The meetings we've held lately at Samotlor, Urengoi and Surgut have shown that machine builders have failed and continue to fail to meet the requirements of oil and gas workers.

Progressive methods of mechanized production are being introduced at an extremely slow pace, the technical standard at most oilfields is insufficient and there are many incidents of equipment and machinery malfunctions.

In the past few years the pioneer traditions of the first Tyumen oil explorers have somehow become tarnished. This has occurred apparently because the ministerial department, *Glavtyumenneftegaz*, has gone from a setter of technical policy to a secondary link between its producing associations and the ministry and has become a trouble-shooting organization.

Yet, in the Tyumen and Tomsk Regions an instructive experience does exist. There are quite a few outstanding labor accomplishments on the record of the *Yuganskneftegaz*, *Tomskneft* and *Nadymgazprom* production amalgamations, of the *Severtruboprovodstroi* trust, of the second Surgut drilling administration and some other work collectives. There are drilling teams in the Tyumen Region with a footage rate of over 100,000 meters per annum, which is nearly twice the average figure for the Region. The best repair teams handle up to three capital and thirteen maintenance repairs per month, which is more than fifty per cent higher than the average figure. Regrettably, all this good experience accumulated by the national oil industry has not yet become standard practice for all Siberian oil teams.

A large share of the blame for the situation in the West Siberian region lies with specialized oil science. For years research organizations of the industry have been spending nearly their entire potential justifying this situation. But research institutes are not meant to be defense counsels under their respective departments. Their task is to look in a creative manner for ways of upgrading the efficiency of production, to promote scientific and technological progress and foresee the industry's future. Here, in the country's main oil and gas region, there is not a single research and production association.

The lessons of the oilmen should be learned well by others so as not to repeat such mistakes. This refers primarily to the executive staff of the gas industry. So far, the industry seems to be doing well enough. I have visited the main gas fields of the region around Urengoi (Western Siberia). The rates and scope of their development are indeed impressive. But when one takes a closer look at things, he discovers that here, too, the putting into operation of new production capacities, road construction, and the development of the repair network are lagging and the standard of automation is low. To obtain the required amount of gas production, work teams exceed the preset extraction quotas for the operational wells.

The Urengoi fields will soon reach their maximum production level. From then on, all additional output will have to be received from Yamburg. But to make that possible the gas fields must first be properly organized there, and this job is not being done quickly enough either.

Principally responsible for the production situation in the region are the oil and gas workers. We must not forget, however, that their successes or failures depend on the work attitudes of all those who have a part to play in the development of the West Siberian complex, above all on geologists, construction and power workers and machine builders.

Geologists must drastically increase the efficiency of their work. They have found themselves in debt to the oilmen. Over the past decade, the backup of oil production in the region with explored reserves has substantially diminished and now stands at the average level for the whole industry. There is a noticeable decline in the potential for an accelerated buildup of oil production in the region. This means that the Ministry of Geology should take a better account of the recommendations of scientists in outlining the directions and scope of prospecting.

The development of the local oil and gas complex is also strongly affected by the inadequate performance of the power industry. Insufficient reliability in power supply leads to huge oil and gas losses and arouses well-justified criticism on the part of the working people.

The meetings and conversations at Surgut indicate that the builders of power stations can work at a high pace and ensure good quality. But because of the lack of necessary equipment, there is a danger that the deadline for the commissioning of the third power unit will not be met. This means they must be helped.

Now a few words about the problems of capital construction in the region. Its current scope is really unprecedented. The volume of work done here is equivalent to building two Volzhsky Auto Factories every year or one BAM railroad every two years. It is common knowledge that Siberians are the initiators of the progressive modular method of building industrial projects. And yet, the present situation in capital construction hinders the solution of many important problems. The approach of the executive staff of the USSR State Committee for Construction, of the construction ministries and the ministries which are their customers lacks scale.

Each time new tasks arise in the development of the oil and gas complex, we must take urgent steps and agree to considerable additional outlays. Now, too, when the need has arisen for intensive development of gas deposits in areas beyond the Arctic Circle by using special super units, *Minneftegazstroi* has again proved unprepared to handle the task.

The necessary pace cannot be attained with belated preparations, particularly now that the construction of the West Siberian complex is entering a more responsible stage. In the next five-year plan period, the scope of building and assembly work is to grow considerably. This means that a program of construction, enormous even by the yardsticks of this country, is to be realized.

But we must take into consideration not only the scope of capital construction, but also the quality and, generally speaking, reliability of everything that we are contemplating, planning, building and developing. This implies security, efficiency and durability. This holds true for the development of new areas as well.

To attain a faster rate of construction work, it is essential to consider once again the question of supplying builders with the necessary equipment and enlarging the scale of work to improve living conditions, first and foremost the housing facilities of the builders themselves.

I would like to point out yet another lesson we should draw from the experience of developing mineral resources in the Tyumen Region. The successes achieved have made some people complacent. Perhaps to save face, or for some other reasons, some leaders were unable or unwilling to realistically assess the true state of affairs and promptly report to the Central Committee and the government. That won't do, Comrades. It is difficult to manage things correctly without receiving objective information. Such an approach is bound to lead to new errors and miscalculations. And with the enormous scale of work this may result in great losses.

In this connection, I think it is appropriate to remind you of what Lenin taught us. He reiterated more than once that we should always and in everything base ourselves on truth, however unpleasant it might be. Any embellishment can only harm our great cause. This behest of Lenin should become a norm of our life.

Consideration for people, concern for them is the main line

of our policy. And for the newly developed areas it acquires special significance. The Tyumen Regional Party Committee seems to realize this, but evidently not in full. The Regional Party Committee and the ministries concerned should treat the tasks of creating normal living conditions for people as most important activities.

New and higher standards of organization of all the work here should correspond to the new and more complex stage in the further development of Siberia. There are necessary prerequisites for this. Tyumen has steeled, experienced cadres devoted to the Party's cause. There is an efficient contingent of many thousands of Communists working here. It is within the powers of such a collective to fulfill the tasks set.

Here, in the center of the vast West Siberian territory, I would like to comment briefly on the problems of the economic and social development of the country's eastern areas in general.

The accelerated development of the productive forces of Siberia and the Soviet Far East is an important element of the Party's economic strategy.

Today Siberia has a highly developed industry and agriculture, grand projects, big economic complexes. It is the main energy supply source of the country. It also has dozens of large modern cities and major, world-famous scientific and cultural centers.

But for all the current significance of Siberia and the Far East for the future of the country, we are all well aware that tomorrow the role of this region will increase immeasurably.

Therefore, in striving to accomplish the most urgent tasks, we must today also look far ahead, literally into the next century. We must have clear perceptions about how to use most rationally and effectively the enormous production and economic potential of Siberia.

It is from this angle that the recent All-Union Conference held in Novosibirsk on productive forces development and the acceleration of scientific and technological progress in Siberia approached this question. The CPSU Central Committee supports the ideas expressed at it concerning the need to transfer to an intensive method of production in Siberia, to extract raw materials from greater depth and exhaustively process them, and to concentrate here an increasing share of the national output of such energy-intensive branches as the iron and steel, nonferrous metal, chemical, petrochemical, microbiological and pulp-and-paper industries and the production of effective building materials.

The proposals to accelerate the development and the reorientation of mechanical engineering plants and relieve them of the production of relatively labor-intensive goods that have little to do with the principal needs of the region deserve the closest attention.

The Politburo has assigned the State Planning Committee, the Academy of Sciences, the State Committee for Science and Technology, USSR ministries and departments and the Russian Federation Council of Ministers to consider and use the conference's recommendations in drafting the Guidelines for the Economic and Social Development of the USSR for the Twelfth Five-Year Plan Period and the Period Ending in the Year 2000.

The rate of economic growth is the key to the future of Siberia and of the entire country.

In short, in order to maintain stable economic growth rates we need a well-thought-out production organization which takes due account not only of today's tasks but also of the long-term tasks of the region and the needs of the country as a whole.

This brings me to a number of other very acute problems for the Siberian and Far Eastern economy.

One of the best ways to raise the effectiveness of capital investment in extracting industries is a shift to the extraction of raw materials at great depth and to effectively process them on site. It is necessary to set aim for the development of mutually supplementary production facilities here. We have already accumulated such experience. Highly effective territorial-industrial complexes have already been set up and are operating in the country. They allow for having a fifteen to twenty per cent savings on capital outlays and considerable reduction in operating costs.

Understandably, all this is directly related to the rational utilization of energy and raw material resources. In order to fully grasp the scale and importance of this problem, it is enough to consider that the expenditure of fuel and raw materials exceeds half the production costs of the country's social product. What's more, the industries producing raw materials and fuel are the most capital and labor intensive. This makes it clear why the changeover to an active resource-saving policy is of paramount importance for the intensification of the national economy and the accelerated development of our society as a whole.

In this context, I would like to give my full support to the drive for economy and thriftiness which has begun in this country. This subject is well covered by the media, particularly the press, which is certainly useful.

But more could be done. One can see that from the experience of the Ukraine where the rate of reducing material consumption per unit of output in the past four years was two times higher than was planned. Upwards of 500 million tons of secondary resources and waste have been used in industrial production in the Republic, and their total proportion in overall resource consumption has been brought up to twelve per cent, twice the national level.

Here, in Siberia and the Far East, in places of concentrated production of fuel and raw materials, there are the greatest opportunities for their comprehensive utilization. However, a considerable amount of casing-head gas in the Tyumen Region is still consumed in torch flames. We cannot put up with that any longer. The problem of using casing-head gas must be resolved more quickly. Nor can we be satisfied with the way things are in oil refinement extension.

A number of examples of such mismanagement could be mentioned in respect to other industries and production units. But the situation is worst of all, perhaps, as regards the use of timber. The amount of final output produced from a cubic meter of timber in Siberia is half the national average.

We must have a resource-saving regimen dependably planned and organized which must serve as the basis of all our economic activity. By the close of 1986 we must reduce energy consumption per unit of the national income by 3.2 per cent and metal consumption, by 3 per cent. This is a very difficult task. We have never yet had such a rate of resource-saving.

We cannot and shall not support the managers who adhere to the earlier modes of operation and to outdated standards and who make increased production growth rates dependent on the availability of additional material resources.

Now, there is another thing deserving special attention. During the current five-year period, the growth rates of circulating capital in stock have been outpacing those of production. The diversion of this capital from national economic turnover completely eats up all that was gained through the saving of material resources.

We must maintain higher rates of the development of science in Siberia and the Far East. We can all clearly see the perspicacity of the decisions made earlier to set up the Siberian branch and the Far Eastern center of the Academy of Sciences and Siberian branches of the Academies of Agricultural and Medical Sciences. The results of the development of Siberian science are self-evident. They are evident here in the Tyumen Region, on the Baikal-Amur Railroad construction project and in other regions.

The task now is to build up research efforts within the framework of the Academy of Sciences and its specialized branches and at institutes of higher learning while strengthening their material and production base and further focussing their efforts on the development of the productive forces of the country's eastern regions.

In Siberia, as in other regions of the country, scientific and technological progress will be a powerful lever of economic development. But a lever must have a point of support, as is known. Capital construction is such a point of support, but unfortunately, it is still our weak spot.

Siberia is rich in local building materials, but their production is not properly organized. The region's requirements for reinforced-concrete construction units, brick and non-ore materials are not fully satisfied and pre-fab housing construction is poorly developed. In accordance with the resolution of the CPSU Central Committee and the USSR Council of Ministers on the further industrializing of capital construction, at least one-third of the production of advanced materials should be arranged in the eastern part of the country.

Local economic executives and specialists could easily resolve the problem. They need no particular directives for it, only appropriate interest in the matter. This is also a matter of the greatest relevance to our economic bodies—the State Planning Committee, the Ministry of Finance and the State Supplies Committee. The financing and crediting of material reserves must be put under strict control. But we should also analyze why the work collectives that shun the resource-saving drive are so easily getting away with it.

Thecountry'sforemostworkcollectivesinitiatedadrivetowork for at least two days this year on saved materials, fuel and electricity. Pledges of this type have been taken almost everywhere. However, they were not backed up everywhere by adequate economic, organizational and educational efforts. Working side by side with those who have already worked for one or two days on saved resources are dozens and even hundreds of enterprises and organizations which fail even to keep within the planned quotas of materials consumption.

True, the development and introduction of resource-saving technology and methods of production should play a very important and progressive role in our drive to economize. We have many untapped scientific and technological reserves here. However, wasteful technologies are still being used on a massive scale.

It is more important for Siberia than for any other region that technological policy should aim at saving labor efforts through more intensive use of electricity, the most advanced technologies and the best machines.

The plan for the country's economic development up to the year 2000 envisages a more than two-fold increase in the volume of construction in Siberia. The necessary condition for its implementation is, above all, technological and organizational modernization of the material base, which would turn construction into a single production process beginning with turning out materials, construction elements and large pre-fab modules and ending with their assembly into completed projects. The management of construction should be upgraded to meet this objective.

Everything I have just said applies not only to the development of production in Siberia and the Far East, but also to social development of the region and people's life there.

Everyone is aware that the living and working conditions in Siberia are special, and this is one of the main lessons of the development of the Tyumen Region. We take this into consideration in our social policy. In the current five-year period dwelling houses, hospitals and preschool child-care institutions were built and municipal and trade services adopted in Siberia and the Far East at a higher rate than in the European part of the country. Regional pay differentials have been introduced or increased, additional pay for uninterrupted record of service has been established for many categories of factory workers and office employees, and other measures have been taken.

All this has had a certain effect. In the past four years the population of the eastern regions of the Russian Federation has grown as a result of the inflow of workers and specialists from other areas of the country. But one cannot ignore another tendency—a sizeable number of people have left this region. So, it is necessary to keep boosting housing construction, improving the supply of the population with foodstuffs and consumer goods, and developing services, public-health facilities and education in Siberia and the Far East.

Of course, this will take effort, resources and time. But Siberia must become not only a big construction site and not only an immense production facility. All of us must keep in mind that all our plans will remain on paper if we fail to make this vast area comfortable for the people's life.

I want to add that each draft of a new construction project in Siberia and the Far East must be well grounded from the social point of view and must envisage better working and living conditions for the people.

And now a few words about one more issue directly relating to making Siberia an area where life will be enjoyable. I mean the necessity of showing a true concern for nature. In Siberia we must act as good proprietors and must not only pursue immediate benefits but also work for preserving the riches and beauty of Siberia for the coming generations.

In conclusion, my visit to your region was short but eventful. It was useful and interesting to see the gigantic work which is being carried out here. Siberia is called a land of the future. This is certainly true, but even today it is adding to the glory, wealth and might of your homeland.

Permit me to wish you and your families success in your work and good health and the best of everything in life to you!

September 6, 1985

24

BUILDING UP
FOOD RESOURCES

This speech was made at the Conference of Leading Party Workers and Managerial Staffs in Tselinograd in the Kazakh Soviet Republic (Central Asia).

W E HAVE invited leaders of the Party and local government bodies of the regions of Kazakhstan and the territories and regions of Siberia and the Urals, a large group of secretaries of rural district Party committees, chairmen of collective farms and state farm managers as well as agrarian scientists to attend this meeting in Tselinograd in order that we may discuss Party and economic affairs.

The April 1985 Plenary Meeting of the Central Committee was followed by direct preparation for the Twenty-seventh CPSU Congress. Intense activity is under way in the country. It involves all work collectives and all spheres of Soviet society. We have to handle many important and complex current and future problems simultaneously.

The review and election campaign in the Party organizations is gathering momentum. Always a major event in the life of the CPSU, especially now, in view of new tasks and the forthcoming Congress, the significance of this campaign increases immeasurably. It is important to conduct reviews and elections in keeping with Party principles, in an atmosphere of constructive criticism and self-criticism, and with the Communists' high sense of responsibility to the people being maintained.

The CPSU Central Committee expects the Party organizations to emerge from this review and election campaign organizationally and ideologically stronger. They have to discard all that hampers their full-scale activity and become capable of inspiring, organizing and leading work collectives to fulfill the tasks now facing the country. Success here will largely depend on those people whom Communists elect to lead Party organizations, particularly on secretaries of primary organizations and Party committees.

The Twenty-seventh CPSU Congress is to adopt a revised edition of the Party program and Guidelines for National Economic and Social Development during the Twelfth Five-Year Plan up to the Period ending in the Year 2000. The drafting of these documents is soon to be completed and, after consideration by a Plenary Meeting of the CPSU Central Committee they will be presented for public discussion. Such a method of drafting documents that involves not only the leading bodies of the Party and the State but all Communists and working people will make it possible, we believe, to bring to the Congress scientifically based proposals enriched by the experience of the entire Party and the entire society.

I would like, however, to make one suggestion. There is no point at all in just waiting for the program and the Guidelines to be adopted by the Congress. The spirit of the times calls for an immediate full-scale effort. The major goals have been established, and we should persistently move ahead, braving all difficulties and checking our actual performance against the Guidelines of the April Plenary Meeting and the subsequent resolutions of the Central Committee. The times we are living in, and the tasks we are facing, compel us to be firm, determined and wise in pursuing the policy we have charted.

One of the major imperatives for us is successfully to combine long-range decision-making with the carrying out of the tasks at hand. Long-range planning and setting of priorities for social and economic development are matters of immense importance. But, at the same time, one should clearly realize that even the most breathtaking plans and finest prospects are worthless unless followed up by an actual effort and by a quest for effective solutions. To do otherwise is day-dreaming. . . .

I would like to emphasize the great significance of the work being done today to achieve the targets of the last year of the Eleventh Five-Year Plan. These are important for creating a reserve for the future and for ensuring a good start of the new five-year plan period which we intend to make a turning point in accelerating our economic and social development.

Every work collective well knows its reserves and what it must do in order to meet the plan targets of this year. A great deal must be done in industry, capital construction, transport, services and trade. Special mention should be made of the tasks facing agriculture. For all our difficulties, we can now count on harvesting more grain than we did last year and on an increase in the output of other farming produce, in particular fodder. There are realistic opportunities for meeting the plan targets in livestock production.

We have now come to a decisive stage in the harvesting campaign. Our ability to fulfill the requirements of the national economy for food and fodder grain depends, to a great extent, on the contribution made by Kazakhstan and the territories and regions of Siberia and the Urals. Aware of this, the Government and the Central Committee of the CPSU have rendered them a lot of help. Now it is your turn to act, Comrades. We hope the Party organizations and working people of Kazakhstan and the regions of Siberia and the Urals will display maximum energy and ability in gathering the harvest and will contribute substantially to the country's grain resources.

It seems symbolic that we are discussing food problems soon after we have discussed in Tyumen the fuel and energy situation. Both are indispensable for building an efficient economy, improving the living standard of the people and building up the country's economic and defense potential.

The creation of a dependable foodstuff base is a matter of the entire Party and the whole nation. The April Plenary Meeting of the CPSU Central Committee firmly pronounced the implementation of the Food Program an urgent task requiring special attention.

I think the May 1982 Plenary Meeting of the Central Committee can be considered a point of reference for analyzing the state of agriculture and the entire agroindustrial complex. A little more than three years have passed since then. The time has shown that we were correct in adopting the Food Program and a set of important decisions aimed at solving crucial problems of the development of the agroindustrial complex. Work is in full swing to carry out the Party's measures. The agricultural machine-building industry is undergoing serious modernization. The targets for the production of mineral fertilizer are close to being met. The area of reclaimed lands has increased considerably.

I would like to make special mention of the large-scale work being done to change the social conditions in the countryside. The construction of housing, service and cultural facilities, and of roads has intensified. All this created favorable conditions for encouraging specialists to stay in the countryside. The implementation of important measures to improve the economic situation at collective and state farms through an increase in purchase prices and bonuses has enhanced their economic position and improved economic performance. The introduction of the cost accounting and team contract methods has favorably influenced people's attitude to work and the results of their work.

Summing up the results of our work since the May 1983 Plenary Meeting, we can say that we have chosen the correct path, learned a great deal, and accomplished a lot.

It is highly significant that there has been a nationwide change of attitude toward the problems related to the development of the agroindustrial complex. The development of agriculture and related industries is now considered a national concern. The demands, needs, and requirements of the countryside are in the focus of attention and are being met promptly.

A legitimate question arises. How has all this affected the performance of collective and state farms and other agroindustrial enterprises and organizations? What has society as a whole gained?

As for the overall agricultural output, the figures for 1983-84 show that the profit increased by 22 billion roubles, or that the output grew by nine per cent as compared to the previous two years of the five-year plan. The output of grain, potatoes, sugar beets, vegetables and fruits also rose. During this same period the average annual production of meat increased by nine per cent, of milk by eight per cent, and of eggs by six per cent. Provided the plan for the current year is fulfilled, state purchases of livestock products will exceed the respective figures for 1982 as follows: meat (live weight) by 2.5 million tons, milk by 9.2 million tons, and eggs by 3.5 billion.

In those years the number of farms working at a loss considerably decreased, and the level of profitability in collective and state farm production on the whole rose. In 1983, the net profit of collective and state farms reached just under 24 billion roubles, and the profitability level equaled nearly twenty-two per cent. In 1984, which was more difficult because of weather conditions, profit stood at 20 billion roubles, and the profitability level at eighteen per cent.

The growth of agricultural output also affected the per capita consumption of foodstuffs. This year the per capita consumption of meat and fish will total 78 kilograms (with fish accounting for 17.7 kilograms), milk 318 kilograms, eggs 260, bread 134 kilograms, potatoes 110 kilograms, vegetables and melons 106 kilograms, fruit and berries 46 kilograms, and sugar nearly 45 kilograms.

What does all this mean? As far as the overall calorific value of our diet is concerned, we are on a level with the world's most developed countries. For the time being, our per capita consumption of meat and fruit is lower than in some countries and is somewhat below the established rational norms of nutrition. From this point of view, meat production is the most important element in the fulfillment of the Food Program. We are lagging behind in this field.

As for other products—milk, eggs, fish, sugar, vegetables and potatoes—the level of their per capita consumption is not lower, and in the case of some products is even higher than in many countries. It corresponds, or is close to, the Food Program targets. The population's requirements for bread and baked products are satisfied with a wide assortment.

Nevertheless, the problem of providing the population with foodstuffs has not yet been fully resolved. For some products demand exceeds supply. The reason for this is that cash incomes have grown faster in our country than the output of foodstuffs. At the same time, state prices of the staple foodstuffs have in effect remained stable for two decades, though their prime cost has been growing. For instance, our shops sell meat at prices which make up one-third or half of its prime cost. At present this difference is made up by a state subsidy which, in the case of meat, amounts to an impressive 20 billion roubles annually.

The fact that in the USSR staple foodstuffs are accessible to all groups of the population is a great achievement. But while noting this, we cannot ignore the issues that worry many Soviet people. Working people address to the Central Committee an increasing number of letters in which they deplore a disrespectful attitude on the part of some people to the work of those who produce grain and other farm products.

"Bread is life," write Comrades Ivanov and Mangalov from the township Magansk in the Krasnoyarsk Territory (Siberia). "It is the wealth, strength and might of our homeland. But what a barbaric attitude to bread one can often see! It is high time this problem is attended to in earnest."

Or here's another letter. "We have nobody starving," says Comrade Sukhanova from Moscow. "One can find loaves of white bread in garbage cans, and the food wastes of canteens are enough to overfeed all livestock."

There are many such letters. Apparently, this subject must be given careful attention both in the work collectives and in the central bodies of government—in fact, in every family too. It is our common task to radically change the attitude to bread and to other foodstuffs.

It is quite obvious, however, that the food problem can be settled largely through persistent work by the Party and by the entire society to develop our agriculture and the agroindustrial complex in general.

In the meantime there are quite a few examples of the increased material, technical and economic opportunities in many regions, territories and republics still being underused. Some managers continue to try and find sources of additional income not in large harvests, higher livestock productivity or thrifty management, but in receiving extra budget allocations and bank credits.

Drawbacks and mistakes have seriously hindered the implementation of the measures designed to impart greater stability to agriculture and, primarily, to crop farming. I should like to stress once more that we won't be able to remake our weather. So in concrete and often difficult conditions the only viable approach is to look for the most effective ways and methods of securing large harvests.

This is the key task of our work in the agroindustrial complex. Its solution is of paramount importance for the regions and territories of Siberia, the Urals and Kazakhstan. Instability in crop farming badly tells on the performance of local collective and state farms. During the four years of the current five-year plan, the targets for most agricultural products in Kazakhstan remained unfulfilled. The republic has a great debt in grain sales to the state. There has been a drop in a number of qualitative indices, and in several districts both field and livestock productivity has declined.

In the past few years, plans for the production and sale of grain to the state have also systematically remained unfulfilled in many Ural and Siberian regions of the Russian Federation. Over the last four years a large debt has accrued in grain sales to the state in many collective and state farms of the Altai and Krasnoyarsk territories and of the Novosibirsk, Orenburg, Kurgan and Chelyabinsk regions. They have also undersupplied large quantities of milk and meat.

Failures in meeting the plan targets for the production and purchase of grain put stress on the satisfaction of the country's needs. This forces us to import grain and thus spend sizable amounts of hard currency. We have set the task of further increasing grain production so as to fully satisfy domestic needs in grain. This is the premise from which the collective and state farms, Party, local government and economic management bodies in the grain-producing republics, territories and regions of the country must proceed in their work.

What does this mean in practical terms? If we single out the main targets, it means that no matter how unfavorable the weather conditions may be, the country has to harvest no less than 200 million tons of grain annually, while a good year should net 250 million or even more. This is what I see as the strategic task of our crop farming for the immediate future!

But the solution of the grain problem does not come down to simply growing more grain. It also includes its rational use.

We cannot compensate for shortcomings in fodder production by the use of large amounts of grain as fodder. This is an inadmissible practice which should not be tolerated. However, it has taken root in many areas. Realizing the great importance of the problem, we should seek a solution to it. Certain lessons on this score have already brought results. In the period from 1983 to 1984 the plans for the procurement of coarse and succulent fodder were not only fulfilled, but overfulfilled. This provided conditions for achieving higher results in the output of livestock products with a lower volume of concentrated fodder. That is why collective and state farms should pay the same attention to fodder production as to grain production. Not less and not worse —these are the two sides of the coin, so to speak. It is necessary to ensure a bumper harvest of fodder crops and a better quality of fodder on the basis of using the modern achievements of science and the experience accumulated at collective and state farms.

I would even say that at present the problem of quality should be given top priority. Control surveys show that due to the low quality of fodder, twenty to thirty per cent of nutrient substances are lost in many regions of the USSR. The excessive consumption of fodder grain is also caused by inadequate measures being taken in some places to eliminate the shortage of fodder protein. On many farms this has already been recognized and vigorous measures taken to solve the protein problem. Some farms, though, rely on the help of state resources. We should support the former and strongly denounce the parasitical attitudes of the latter.

Now that the plans for the next five-year period are being shaped it is very important that at every collective or state farm, in all districts, regions, territories and republics, the problems connected with the increasing of meat resources be thoroughly considered. This is a top priority task. In the final year of the Eleventh Five-Year Plan meat output is expected to increase by two million tons (slaughter weight) as compared with 1980. In order to meet the targets of the Food Program we must double this figure during the Twelfth Five-Year Plan.

On the whole, the targets set for the output of grain, fodder, meat, milk and other agricultural produce show that intensive work lies ahead in the next five-year plan. This should be completely understood by all workers of the agroindustrial complex and, above all, by our leading cadres.

These questions arise: How can we reach such targets and do we have all the necessary conditions for this? It is not rhetoric, but an earnest answer to say definitely on behalf of the Central Committee of the Party that today we have such possibilities and such conditions. This is evidenced by the work done by thousands of collective and state farms in a number of territories and regions since the May 1982 Plenary Meeting of the CPSU Central Committee.

At present a task of top priority is to ensure high returns in agriculture and the agroindustrial complex as a whole. The level of returns per unit of assets in the countryside remains low so far. In the two years following the May 1982 Plenary Meeting of the Central Committee, the production assets of collective farms and state farms in the Kurgan Region have increased by almost thirteen per cent, while gross agricultural output has fallen there by twelve per cent. A similar picture obtains in the Kustanai Region, where the increment in basic production assets during the same period was up fourteen per cent, while the output of products diminished. A decline in agricultural production, despite a noticeable increase in fixed assets per worker, has taken place in a number of other regions of the Russian Federation, the Ukraine, Kazakhstan and Uzbekistan.

The basic link which we must mend in order to fulfill the whole range of practical tasks facing us in the countryside is the proper organization of production and labor at collective and state farms, and all enterprises of the agroindustrial complex. Wide use must be made of the available experience of highly productive, efficient work. Everything depends here on the activity of leading cadres, Party, government and economic bodies, and not on additional capital investments.

I would like to dwell on a few of the practical matters in greater detail.

First, what is needed is more boldness in going over to new and advanced technologies, to more effective forms of using material resources and then to concentrate them primarily in those areas where they can yield the highest returns. It is essential for us during the next five-year period to give the utmost importance to growing grain crops with the application of intensive methods.

About 17 million hectares of wheat and nearly all grain corn is being cultivated according to intensive methods this year. Despite erratic weather, the yield gain is quite impressive. As the data of the Ministry of Agriculture and the USSR Academy of Agricultural Sciences show, farms obtain from four to five tons of grain per hectare in many areas, or 1.5 to 2 tons more than with the usual technology.

The new methods are gaining ever firmer ground. Following proposals from the localities, grain crops will be sown according to intensive methods on an area of over 31 million hectares for the 1986 harvest. Of this area, almost 4 million hectares will be sown in corn. In the near future, given good preceding years, we can extend the use of intensive methods to an area of not less than 60 million hectares. It is here that fertilizers, machinery and other resources should be primarily concentrated, so as to guarantee high yields and impart the necessary stability to grain production.

But there is more to it than that. We have had a brief meeting with scientists today. The results of this discussion may be summed up as follows: The paramount issue at this stage is the observance of technological standards in the fields. In agriculture the same kind of technological discipline is required as, for example, in the smelting of steel or iron. A slight error, and the metal will be of a different quality. This is the stage of work in the fields that we have approached. In order to obtain the maximum effect through the use of intensive methods, skilled personnel is indispensable. But we have not everywhere achieved an adequate level of professional training.

Many of our farmers are used to working in the following way: They do the sowing and then harvest what has grown. Just that and nothing more. With intensive methods you can't work that way. Using these methods, the cultivation of crops requires much skill and experience of a farmer. This is why personnel should be properly trained, for without thorough knowledge the situation won't improve. This, Comrades, is the reliable way of obtaining high and stable yields. The time of general instructions and slogans is gone. Party committees must keep this enormously important matter under their daily control and promote in every way the use of intensive methods, relying on science and advanced experience.

Secondly, the potential of scientifically-based crop-farming systems is still being inadequately used in many places. Such systems have been worked out for every zone, and, in fact, for every farm. This is an important means of raising soil fertility. Also, one must remember that the neglect of any of the elements of the crop-farming system disrupts the entire cycle in the battle for a good harvest and may bring the expenditure of labor and money to naught. I would like to make special mention of fallow land. Or, to be more precise, of the attitude toward it. Remember the hot debates that went on just a few years ago about whether or not to maintain fallow land. Science and the point of view based on the data of science won in the end. Now we have about 22 million hectares lying fallow. In the main grain-producing regions of Kazakhstan, Siberia and the Urals they occupy 15-20 per cent of plowland.

Terentii Maltsev, who is present here, used every occasion to remind me of this method saying that the matter should be brought to its logical conclusion. If the land lying fallow in Siberia and in the upturned virgin land areas of Kazakhstan makes up less than twenty per cent, we'd rather have none at all.

We have now either attained or come near to attaining this level. But the results are quite varied and have to be analyzed thoroughly. There is plenty of evidence to show that in arid years well-prepared and properly cultivated fallow land has produced double or triple the harvest of the land that did not lie fallow. This was particularly noticeable in bad years. The quality of grain has also been far better than in other fields. But that has not been the case everywhere. For example, even in such major grain-producing areas as the Omsk, Saratov, Orenburg and Tselinograd regions, or the Altai Territory, the extension of the land left to lie fallow has not yet ensured a proper growth of gross grain harvests.

What is the matter? It is that some land left to lie fallow has not had proper handling. This is not a new problem. We have spoken about it more than once. In one case the fallow land was not plowed up in good time, in another it was left uncultivated and free to grow over with weeds. Now what about district and regional agroindustrial amalgamations, agricultural specialists, and zonal research institutes? And, above all, Comrades, how can an agronomist look indifferently at all this? The land is a matter of his vital concern, of his honor and conscience as a specialist and lawmaker in the fields!

Next. It is obvious to all of us that in the specific conditions of our country, with its pronounced continental climate and oft-recurring droughts, it is impossible to have stable agricultural production with ameliorated, above all, irrigated lands.

We have accomplished much by carrying out a sweeping program of agricultural land improvement. This work will be further expanded under plans already worked out and adopted. This firm line of ours was reaffirmed at the CPSU Central Committee Plenary Meeting in October 1984.

Yet a top priority of today is not to enlarge the area of ameliorated land but to use it effectively. The harvests obtained so far do not correspond either to the expenses we have incurred or to the actual potentialities of the improved lands. All that the Ministries of Agriculture, Land Reclamation and Water Management and the USSR Academy of Agricultural Sciences have, in fact, been doing so far is to take note of this unsatisfactory state of affairs. There have been enough instructions in this respect, yet the heads of the above-mentioned organizations have failed to show a proper Party sense of responsibility for implementing the decisions of the CPSU Central Committee and the Government.

One can sometimes hear this kind of reasoning: It is enough

to have irrigated lands and good harvests will come automatically. This is something, you know, that reminds me of the reasoning of die-hard partisans of extensive farming. In matters relating to the use of irrigated lands we can least of all afford to wait for something to turn up automatically. In irrigated and ameliorated lands it is a must to get crops cultivated by intensive methods. Furthermore, the measures for a radical improvement of the ameliorated arable land should be taken without any delay. That is where the capital investments on hand must be used, first and foremost. This is the demand of the CPSU Central Committee and the Government, and it must be met unfailingly.

Fourth, the problems of livestock farming. We have to admit that, despite certain effort, scientific and technological progress so far has had little effect on this sector. Some high-ranking officials and experts still try to resolve the problems of boosting the output of meat, milk and other products through the use of extensive development factors.

Several years ago, when we emphasized as the main trend in livestock farming qualitative improvement and higher productivity, rather than growth of livestock population, many showed no support for this idea or were even opposed to it. Practice has shown, however, that our approach is justified. And it cannot be otherwise. This has been proven by the practice on many advanced farms. In the past two or three years, when the number of cows and other livestock in the country did not effectively increase, and the number of cows even decreased, there was a rise, not sharp but nonetheless steady, in the output and state procurement of livestock products.

We must continue to concentrate not on a growth of the livestock population, as this involves great expenditure for the construction of new farms as well as maintenance by the farm personnel, but on the determined introduction of intensive methods of livestock output. It is a fair guess that there will continue to be districts and even regions where livestock population should be increased if the production of fodder develops at a priority rate there. But the chief attention should be given to intensifying livestock farming.

If the delivered weight of each head of cattle is increased by at least fifty kilograms, we shall obtain an additional 1.5 million tons of meat in live weight, with the number of cattle remaining unchanged. This would be far cheaper and economically more efficient than obtaining the same additional amount of meat through a growth of the cattle population which would then have to be increased by nearly five million head.

Our dairy farming also needs a new approach. We must more actively avail ourselves of the opportunities opened up by breeding, by introducing new technologies and balanced-out feeding methods. These are the main prerequisites for high productivity. If today we were to obtain an average of 3,000 kilograms of milk from each cow of the existing number of cows in the country we would not know what to do with the surplus.

The questions of intensifying poultry and livestock farming and raising their productivity are particularly pressing in the regions and territories of Siberia and Kazakhstan and should be given the greatest attention.

The problem of improving storage and processing of farm produce is a most important problem of the Twelfth Five-Year Plan. The central bodies, which are responsible for furnishing the material and technological base for storage and processing, and the local Party and government organizations, which should look for ways of solving this problem, must be criticized. There is a need to ensure faster rates of development of the third sphere of the agroindustrial complex, particularly machine building for the food industry.

Participation of other ministries is indispensable for the solution of this problem. Local Party organizations and government bodies must work harder to carry out this task of major importance for the whole state and determine what exactly must and can be done locally to modernize and retool food, meat and dairy industry enterprises, vegetable storehouses and plants that manufacture and assemble refrigeration equipment.

Comrades, I would like to emphasize that there are problems whose solution entirely depends on you. Is it really a problem for big cities and regional and territorial centers, with their vast industrial potential and dozens of building organizations, to build facilities necessary for storing and marketing fruits and vegetables? I have been told, for example, that the system of delivering fruits and vegetables to shops directly from the fields works well in Tselinograd. It is a very important undertaking. The failure to make such systems work in some places is the result of an irresponsible attitude rather than difficulties. This is the only way of putting it, because this problem affects people's day-to-day needs and dampens the efforts to raise people's standard of living.

Building ministries should not push the construction and modernization of food industry enterprises into the background. I hope the builders will draw appropriate conclusions from this discussion.

There is one more question. The technological and organizational changes under way in agriculture and related industries require new attitudes toward the use of our research institutions' potentialities. It goes without saying that agricultural science has done and continues to do a great deal, of course. This is well known. But we cannot rest on our laurels.

The Central Committee has set the task of intensifying research efforts. Science must become a true catalyst of progress in the countryside. What is needed here is to drastically raise the level and enhance the effectiveness of research.

We are now passing through a stage where more vigorous efforts to promote the key directions of scientific and technological progress and fundamental research toward solving the pressing problems of biology and biotechnology are imperative. The Politburo has recently examined this issue and has passed a detailed resolution on it. The latest findings of scientists, the new achievements in this field, enable us to boost sharply the intensity of the major biological processes.

Progressive directions and modern patterns and methods of research open up vast opportunities for selection. The application of genetic and cell-engineering methods can dramatically speed up the development of new plant varieties in crop farming which are resistant to diseases, droughts and frost and are well adapted to the specific natural conditions of each region. This applies also to the breeding of new, more productive breeds of livestock and poultry.

As the problems of scientific support for agriculture stand now, they require the broad interaction of experts from various fields of knowledge. So here I would like to appeal to the USSR Academy of Sciences to step up its cooperation with the USSR Academy of Agricultural Sciences and with other research institutions of an agroindustrial orientation. Intensive integration of fundamental science with research institutions of the agroindustrial complex is a major source of improving the standards of agricultural science and the effectiveness of its influence on agricultural production.

Greater attention should be paid to the introduction of research findings into practice. This can take various forms. Experience shows, however, that the most rational form of all is that of research and production associations. This has been tested and borne out by many years of practice. . . .

We are unanimous in understanding the need for the earliest possible accomplishment of the tasks facing the agroindustrial complex. I have no doubt that we all agree that this requires a great amount of organizational and political work. The answer to the question of how to do this work more efficiently can be found in the decisions of the April 1985 Plenary Meeting, in the materials of the conference in the CPSU Central Committee on the problems of scientific and technological progress and in other Party documents. It is our duty to put into effect the ideas, instructions and conclusions outlined in these documents, resolutely and consistently.

What is needed is an enterprising effort in the nation's agrarian sector. This applies to all cadres—Party, government, managerial and trade union. This applies to Party organizations at all levels.

Resourceful, well-thought-out work of Party organizations will enable us to tap deep-lying reserves of production and secure high returns on the productive, economic and manpower potential that has been created in the countryside. That is exactly what now has to be regarded as a matter of top priority. I would like to refer in this context to the role of our rural district Party committees. Currently there are 3,200 of them. They are in charge of over 49,000 collective farm and state farm Party organizations. There are 6,500,000 Communists in the countryside, which is over one-third of our entire Party membership. This is a force, a vanguard that can do really great things, both in production and in social development. The CPSU Central Committee highly appreciates the activities of this large contingent of our Party and the contribution the Party committees make toward carrying out the Party's political strategy and the Food Program in particular.

There is, however, something I have to criticize. An inquiry by the corresponding Central Committee departments into the operation of a number of regional Party organizations has shown that many district Party Committees are slow in reorganizing their work and sometimes forget that a Party committee is a body of political leadership.

Some district committees veer off the correct path. It is difficult at times to distinguish the forms and methods of the work of a Party committee from those of an economic governmental body. Not all committees give proper attention to upgrading ideological work.

Work with personnel is of immense importance to a rural district committee. Collective farm and state farm managers are indeed our gold mine. We must highly value and raise the prestige of the difficult jobs of chairmen and managers in farms, so as to have a stable and capable staff of economic leaders in each district, region, territory and republic. . . .

This conference and counsel, preceding the forthcoming Party Congress and the beginning of the next five-year plan, are of particular significance not only to this major agricultural region but to all of our country and to our entire society. Kazakhstan, Siberia, and the Urals have the necessary conditions for implementing grain procurement plans successfully and making a tangible contribution to the nation's food resources. That will be a good present for the Twenty-seventh Congress.

September 7, 1985

25

THE UNDYING
TRADITIONS
OF LABOR

This speech was made at the meeting of the CPSU Central Committee with veterans of the Stakhanovite movement, advanced workers and innovators of production.

Dear Comrades,

On behalf of the Central Committee of the CPSU, allow me to cordially welcome you, the veteran workers who laid the foundations of the Stakhanovite movement, which embodied the valor, honor and heroism of working people, as well as those of the front rank and the innovators of production who have been worthily upholding the undying traditions of labor.

There is a good occasion for this meeting. Half a century has passed since the pioneering effort of Stakhanov sparked off a movement of millions of working people. I think it is correct not only to recall the exciting events of those days, but to discuss how we might best use the mobilizing potentialities of socialist competition to resolve the urgent problems of today.

The Stakhanovite movement has acquired great and undiminishing significance. It was a vivid demonstration, as Vladimir Lenin described, of the experience of the early communist subbotniks, of ". . . the conscious and voluntary initiative of the workers in developing the productivity of labor, in adopting a new labor discipline, in creating socialist conditions of economy and life." [V. I. Lenin, *Collected Works,* Fourth edition, vol. 29, pp. 423-424.]

What a profound and vast definition, Comrades, and how consonant it is with our priorities at this turning point!

The Stakhanovite movement was born in unforgettable years. The young Soviet State, racing against time, was carrying out its industrialization program in leaps and bounds. It had to be quick in raising labor efficiency, finding new forms of organization and making full use of the opportunities stemming from technical reconstruction and from the modernization of the material base of production.

The movement reflected the new attitude to work which Maxim Gorky described as a fiery explosion of mass energy. A sweeping outburst of the creative powers of a young nation, its working class and peasantry, took place. It did not come as a surprise, of course, for it had been prepared by the entire development of a new type of social relations and by the consistent work of the Party.

Quite a few years have passed since then, but today we still talk of the pace setters of the Stakhanovite movement with a feeling of admiration and pride. Each and every one of them was a remarkable and talented person, and all of them came from the very heart of the people—the coal miners Alexei Stakhanov and Nikita Izotov, the smith Alexander Busygin, the miner and Party organizer Konstantin Petrov, the steelworker Makar Mazai, the milling-machine operator Ivan Gudov, the engine driver Pyotr Krivonos, the shoemaker Nikolai Smetanin, the textile workers Yevdokia Vinogradova and Maria Vinogradova, the combine operator Konstantin Borin, the tractor drivers Pasha Angelina and Praskovya Kovardak, the sugar beet growers Maria Demchenko and Marina Gnatenko, to name just a few.

To be a Stakhanovite or work like Stakhanov means to display initiative, strive for progress and fight everything that has become outdated and obsolete. The Stakhanovite movement as both a social and moral phenomenon revealed the inner beauty of the new man. The pioneers of this movement became national heroes. They set examples for workers, farmers, intellectuals and young people.

I am saying this not only because I want to pay a tribute to history. When one looks at the veteran Stakhanovites and at the advanced workers of today who are sitting in this hall, one can't help thinking of the organic connection between various generations and of the continuity of socialist traditions. Neither technology nor people today are what they were half a century ago, but the traditions of the Stakhanovite movement have not disappeared or become a thing of the past. The indomitable spirit of innovation characteristic of the Stakhanovite trailblazers, with their determination to use technology to full capacity and their daring is eliminating antiquated practices and psychological ruts are particularly consonant with our times.

The Party has now embarked on a road of speeding up the country's social and economic development, the rate of scientific and technological progress and fostering discipline and order in everything. We have to make our economy more dynamic, intensify it and ensure maximum efficiency of production. This policy answers, or to be more exact, fully reflects the aspirations and sentiments of the working people.

Our plans and our short- and long-term policy will be conclusively determined by the Twenty-Seventh Congress of the Communist Party of the Soviet Union. However, we know basically even now how our economy should develop in the Twelfth five-year plan period and up until the beginning of the Third Millennium. We know what links should be considered of decisive importance and where we should exert the greatest effort. During the next three five-year periods we have to ensure growth in industrial output equal to the industrial potential built up during all the preceding postrevolutionary years. Moreover, the pivotal point is that we should do so through intensification of the economy.

Life itself has set this pace. It is also prompted by the need to raise the Soviet people's standard of living and maintain the country's defense at a level that absolutely ensures the security of this country and its allies. In short, in keeping with the principle of policy advanced by Lenin, we have had to make a decisive historic choice and the Party has made it. It has set the task of achieving a qualitatively new state of society through substantial acceleration of social and economic progress. We shall take this path and shall keep to it undeviatingly and consistently. We must focus now on the practical implementation of elaborated measures, on concrete jobs, on the hard day-to-day work of everyone without exception, be he or she a worker, farmer, a specialist, a scientist or a plant or industry manager.

Recently I visited an oil- and gas-bearing region of Western Siberia and the virgin land areas of Kazakhstan. My conversations with workers and specialists were serious and frank. The main conclusion that can be drawn from them is that Soviet workers, farmers, engineers and scientists well realize their responsibility for tackling the problems that face the country. There is clear understanding of the need not merely to move forward but to make a real breakthrough along the entire frontier of scientific and technological progress and achieve a radical change in the development of the economy.

Against the background of these new tasks, people are becoming noticeably more active and more interested in change. They are looking for new solutions to problems and for more effective methods of organizing socialist competition. The mass movements initiated by working people in recent years bear witness to this.

Thus work collectives in Moscow and Leningrad are competing to achieve the entire increase in output through technical progress and a maximum use of equipment. Machine builders in the Ukraine have undertaken to attain all of the output increase in the Twelfth five-year period without increasing consumption of ferrous rolled products or of the number of workers employed. The metallurgical workers of the cities of Lipetsk, Nizhni Tagil and Cherepovets are improving their performance through fuller use of facilities and secondary resources and through improving the quality of the product. Quite a few enterprises are getting good final results through more efficient certification of work places and more rational use of them. The initiative of the work collectives, which have decided to work for no less than two days this year on saved raw materials, has been supported all across the country.

I would like to dwell particularly on the important initiative of the Volzhsky Car Amalgamation, which has been approved by the CPSU Central Committee. In a nutshell, that work collective has drafted concrete proposals aimed at raising the efficacy of production and the quality of output, which are both much higher than the control targets for the Twelfth five-year plan period fixed by their ministry. It has been decided to drastically raise the productivity of labor and reduce the expenditure of metal per car and the amount of the fuel used. Meanwhile the guaranteed operative life span of new car models is to be increased by fifty per cent. The work collective has asked that its proposal be included in the State Plan.

It is worth noting that the acceleration of the Volzhsky Car

Amalgamation's work is to a great extent based on the experience of introducing a self-supporting basis throughout, from the enterprise level to that of each team in each work place. This is a worthy response to the Party's call to put all reserves at the service of the national economy. It also provides an example of a proprietory interest in work.

As we can see, the vanguard work collectives today are primarily orienting themselves toward raising the quality of their production. This is being achieved by introducing new machinery and technologies, saving resources, fulfilling all the obligations stipulated by agreements and raising the efficacy of production. It goes without saying that I single out only some aspects of emulation and that its forms are as diversified as life.

Of paramount importance is, of course, turning the workers into masters of production and increasing their awareness of the range and novelty of the contemporary tasks. Emulation is a most important means of developing working people's creativity. It is a principal means by which the Soviet citizen can rise and fulfill himself, display his abilities, talents and civic qualities and gain social recognition.

In short, we have made headway and the early results are in evidence. But this is only the beginning of important work. We are facing tasks of an enormous scale, which are to be fulfilled consistently and undeviatingly. They concern all spheres of life and demand from all sectors of management the highest degree of responsibility. We shall continue to pursue perseveringly and steadily the policy of orienting economic executives toward new approaches in compliance with demands put forward by the Party.

But the success of the undertaking, Comrades, ultimately depends on the performance of work collectives—in production associations and enterprises, workshops and teams, and at individual work places. This is achieved through the energy, intellectual power and, I would say, the enthusiasm and honest and conscientious attitude of every worker. Conscientious work for the common good, strict observance of discipline, responsibility and initiative and concern for the interests of the state as one's own interests—these are in essence the demands put on every-one.

For these purposes, all levers—economic and social, and all incentives, materials and moral—should be brought into play. At the same time, I would like to draw special attention to the importance of an incentive that cannot be measured in terms of money. The experience of the past years and the present shows how important it is to take note of, support and praise the conscientious work done by workers, collective farmers, special-ists and scientists—all of whom add to the glory of our home-land.

For those marching in the front ranks it is not always easy to carry the load. Figuratively speaking, the wind is not always blowing in the right direction. The front-runners have to break down the obsolete traditions, to overcome inertness or misunder-standing. But every innovator is the glory and pride of the nation, a great asset to socialist society. Such people must be supported. Their names and deeds should be made known coun-trywide to every work collective.

While encouraging initiative and highly productive work in every way possible, it is essential to be simultaneously strict and exacting toward those who work inefficiently, who violate labor discipline and technological rules, who turn out defective goods. In letters received by the Central Committee, working people suggest that more effective legal, material, administrative and other penalties should be used against those who do not want to work conscientiously. This is fair, and this is how we must act. Indeed, the new mechanism of economic management, being adopted by an increasingly greater number of enterprises and sectors of the economy, pursues that aim.

The Central Committee expects workers, farmers, techni-cians and engineers, office employees and intellectuals to dis-play creativity and spare no effort for ensuring that the accelera-tion of the country's socioeconomic development becomes a reality and that the life of the Soviet people is made materially and culturally even richer, fuller and more meaningful.

Comrades! Vladimir Lenin considered very important the

ability ". . . to arouse both *competition* and *initiative among the masses*, so that they set about the job *straightaway*." [V. I. Lenin, *Collected Works*, vol. 35, p. 467.] Practically all working people are involved in socialist emulation today. But I think that the effect of the socialist emulation movement is not always what it should be. The reasons for this vary. One of the main ones is that the forms and methods of competition by no means always fully match the nature of the present stage of economic development. In many work collectives, socialist emulation proceeds its own way, without a strong or close connection with efforts to shift the economy to intensive lines, to boost scientific and technological progress, rebuild the economic mechanism and introduce the collective forms of labor organization on a large scale.

This situation requires drastic change. Now that we have begun identifying reserves and most effectively utilizing everything we have, let us take a fresh look from this angle at emulation itself as well. On the whole, it still lacks a clearer orientation toward priority aims: higher productivity and quality of output and more effective resource saving.

Pace, quality, thrift and organization are the main catchwords of the day.

Using this opportunity, I would like to reiterate the need for a significant improvement in output quality. This involves a whole set of questions relating to economics, politics, and morality. Low output quality is the obvious result of squandering public funds as well as human labor. Take, for example, consumer goods. One can understand the buyer who wonders why we know how to make spacecraft and atomic-powered ships, but often produce defective household gadgets, shoes and clothes. And this involves not just financial, but also moral and political losses.

There is no secret about why all this occurs. One of the main reasons is poor adherence to technological standards and not strict enough demand on those responsible for the quality of products. Here a lot depends on the work collectives themselves. We firmly believe that workers and collective farmers, scientists, specialists, engineers and technicians as well as economic executives will launch a drive to make all domestic products as good as their best world counterparts or even better.

Speaking of quality, in no way do I mean to say that the quantitative indicators have lost their significance. Now, as before, we need to produce more grain, vegetables, meat, coal, oil and consumer goods. In some industries output growth will remain an important indicator in labor competition. But it is equally obvious that we cannot expand the production of, say, energy and raw material resources infinitely. We must learn to thriftily use each ton of steel, oil, fertilizer, each kilowatt-hour of electricity, each cubic meter of timber.

This is why competition should include the economical and rational use of labor and material and financial resources. I have already spoken on this subject, but considering that the change for the better is coming slowly, I want to stress once again that economizing, thrift and the most effective use of the production potentials are our immediate reserve and a decisive condition for raising the efficiency of the national economy.

We must appreciate each practical step in this direction and bring the squanderers to strict account. For it happens that you see in the shop or the factory yard, posters calling for economizing and thrift while the premises of the factory are littered with scrap metal and machines not installed on time. So, what we see in word differs radically from what we have in deed.

Comrades,

The role of trade unions in coping with the tasks facing our society can hardly be overestimated. The most sacrosanct aspect of their activity is concern. It is a concern for social and cultural needs, working and living conditions and the rest and leisure of the working people. Yet these problems cannot be coped with unless there is a constant and persistent effort for the highest possible level of productivity, discipline and proper organization of production. There is no other way to create wealth but through efficient work. That is why protection of the working people's interests by boosting productivity is the primary duty of trade unions and all work collectives.

To this end, the Law on Work Collectives must be applied more persistently than it currently is. Work collectives become centers where the problems confronting us are focused. They fulfill plans, test new ideas and produce cadres. This is not a passing glance from the top but a thorough study of the situation, an account at grassroots levels, that may help, for example, more effectively introduce team work based on cost accounting. And I mean cost accounting, for there are many teams, but in industry, let's say, only one-fifth of them work on the principle of cost accounting.

In a team, as you no doubt know well, anyone can be in the public eye, and the work collective members themselves assess the degree of each person's involvement in joint work. Here the principles of social justice are better applied in reality in terms of wages and other material and moral incentives. Here it is difficult to hide behind others. The connection between obligations and the end results of production is more visible.

So the trade unions are largely responsible for creating an atmosphere of everyday, painstaking search for reserves in work collectives and an atmosphere of exactingness, both "horizontal" and "vertical" so to say. However, one often gets the impression that a trade union committee has been involved in everything and yet has not singled out the chief areas where its efforts should be exerted. As a result, a good deal of enthusiasm, as often happens in organizing an emulation campaign, is simply wasted "on paper" for "creating" and "planning" the public events involved.

Formalism is the sworn enemy of competition as the direct creative effort of the masses. It is no secret that some obligations are "carbon-copied" and handed to the participants just to sign. Competition targets are fixed without taking into account the specific conditions of an enterprise or an industry. Or take the personal obligations of the participants. They are a good thing in themselves. But why should a worker or engineer in effect copy the list of his official duties and give his word to carry them out? This is a gross distortion of the very idea of competition.

There is another question to be considered. Aren't there too many kinds of competitions and incentives? They do not always have a beneficial effect. The most valuable aspect of competition is the achievement of an excellent performance, the emergence of advanced production know-how and innovating ideas and work methods. Now, if we compare the numerous initiatives with their effect, we are bound to conclude that far from all of them have been thought through well enough.

I believe it is precisely in this area that the work of trade union and economic bodies should be stepped up. It is wrong to have real work substituted for by high-sounding slogans, and real effort by multitudes of far-fetched activities.

There are other urgent issues which must be dealt with. These are responsibility for the organization and technical arrangements involved in emulation and for the economical verification of the pledges, for overcoming the equalization of material incentives among all winners and for building up the prestige of those of the first rank. There must be precise standards of reference by which to judge both success and failure. I trust the participants of this meeting have something to say on this and other matters.

Let me touch now on so complex a problem as alcoholism. The measures which have been taken to combat it are enthusiastically supported by people, although there are some who are displeased. Encouraging results are already in evidence. The consumption of alcoholic drinks has dropped. People have become more intolerant of drunkenness, and there is greater order in the streets of cities and villages, just as there is at the workplaces. The number of traumatic accidents has decreased sharply in the last three months. And this has made it possible to preserve the health of thousands of people, which is the greatest asset of all.

This means that we have not begun such a tremendous effort in vain. We shall perseveringly carry out the plans we have outlined. We understand very well that we have yet a long and difficult job to do to make abstinence a way of life in our society. We have enough patience for that. All the more so since in following this line, the CPSU Central Committee relies on support from all the people and the maturity and strength of public opinion.

Comrades, the Stakhanovite movement has a special distinguishing feature. It was started by young people, none of whom were over thirty. This is natural, for no task of any historical magnitude can be accomplished without young people's vigorous, effective and total involvement. Today as never before it is important to make full use of the energies of the younger generation for carrying out the enormous tasks facing our society.

They sometimes say that today's youth is slow to reach civic maturity. And some people of the older generation even grumble about this. But in the broader picture, we can be satisfied with the Soviet youth of today. Our young men and women are children and grandchildren of those who during the period of industrialization set labor productivity records which were unheard-of at that time, who in the hard war years rose first to the attack, covered gunports with their bodies and rammed the enemy warplanes and tanks. They are the children and grandchildren of those who developed the virgin lands and produced oil and gas in the tundra and Siberian taiga. They are our children and grandchildren, our comrades-in-arms who are demonstrating to the entire world the best examples of work, of service and devotion to their homeland. They are building the Baikal-Amur Mainline railroad and new towns, growing grain and loyally defending the borders of our country.

The Party and the people highly appraise Soviet youth's contribution to the building up of socialism and communism. We trust our young people in everything and see to it that they have ample opportunity to demonstrate their worth and display their capabilities in all the spheres of production and public life.

Our socialist cause will gain only if the Party committees and the economic bodies, together with the Komsomol, find ways and means to more fully use the energy and talent, interest in everything new, firm intolerance of routine and conservatism, and healthy ambition of young workers and innovators, engineers and scientists in ways that include emulation. It is also essential that promising specialists be promoted promptly to commanding posts in production, science, management, administration and in culture. This approach is always justified.

Many of you have probably seen the television program in the series "You Can Do This," which dealt with people who make models of cars with their own hands. Among many models shown one stood out. It had been made by two young workers from Leningrad—Dmitry Parfenov who is studying evening courses at an institute, and Gennady Khainov, a graduate of a ship instrument-making technical school. Within three years these two 25-year-olds, in conditions not geared for such work, constructed a car of original design. They have demonstrated their vast technological knowledge and nonstandard thinking. I think it was right that these skilled workers were given a special laboratory to continue their work.

I have specially cited this example to stress that we must take every opportunity to open the way for realizing young people's technical aspirations and to create all necessary conditions for directing their constructive efforts toward accomplishing the tasks of an accelerated socioeconomic development of society. Work is now under way to prepare proposals dealing with these questions, which will be considered by the Party Central Committee.

A year ago the CPSU Central Committee adopted a resolution called: "On Further Improvement in Party Guidance of the Young Communist League (Komsomol) and the Enhancement of its Role in the Communist Education of Youth." Party and Komsomol organizations thoroughly studied this resolution, which undoubtedly helped the Komsomol to boost its activity. The Komsomol has begun to take greater interest in current problems and become less bound by formalism. However, a great deal more has to be done.

What exactly? The Komsomol must persistently make a reality Lenin's urgent request that one should study Communism and study it every day—at one's factory, in the field, in the classroom, in one's laboratory, and be able to carry out everyday work without losing sight of the communist future. The Komsomol must be aware of everything that interests and worries young people. The style and methods of Komsomol work must appeal to them, inspire them and be freed in form and in essence from too many rules and regulations, campaigns and all sorts of trumpery which continue to take much effort and resources.

Comrades, this country has entered a period of tremendous importance. The outcome of the current year plan and the five-year plan as a whole is being decided. Preparations for the coming Party Congress are growing in scale and this determines the pace of life and activity of Party organizations and work collectives and the social atmosphere as a whole.

Now, as the Party analyzes what has been done and works out a policy for the future, it is essential for us to know your opinions about the most urgent problems and your suggestions for solving them. The Central Committee of the Party always listens attentively to all that the workers, collective farmers, specialists and scientists have to say, and checks its policies against the experience of the masses. This cannot be otherwise, for the cause of the Party is the cause of the people.

The Party is convinced that the problems facing society will be tackled successfully. The Party feels confident because it has a clean-cut program of action and relies upon the creative potential of the people, upon the efficiency, discipline, political awareness and professional skills of the working class, the collective farm workers and the intelligentsia. The implementation of the Party's policy will make our homeland even richer and stronger, the people's life even better and our development even more dynamic.

It is worth living, working and fighting for these noble ideals.

*   *   *

The Closing Speech

DEAR Comrades,

I think it has been a pleasure for all of us to meet here. Each of you has had something to tell about because you were at the beginning of the Stakhanovite movement and then vigorously continued to carry it on. You represent a living history of this country.

By your work you have proved that in the long run everything depends on the human being. When we had to do within a historically short period of time what other peoples and nations have done in the course of centuries, and to cope with the immense tasks of building a socialist society, the Soviet people under the guidance of the Communist Party created a powerful industrial base and rapidly developed productive forces. Thanks to this we were able to break the fascist war machine turned against us by imperialism.

That was a result of the self-sacrificing labor effort of all Soviet people. That was the merit of the older generations. Today, on behalf of all the people, we express our great gratitude to those who were the standard-bearers of innovation and of the Stakhanovite movement.

Now that we are marking the fiftieth anniversary of the Stakhanovite movement, we find this nationwide gratitude to be well deserved, for the traditions of those years are undying. Here in this hall veterans are surrounded by young people who will yet have their say and guide others by their personal example.

The Stakhanovite movement continues. This movement, supported by the people—the working class, the farmers, the intellectuals—will live forever. It will always be the Party's base of support in implementing new large-scale tasks. That is why the Central Committee wants not only to maintain everything that has been achieved through the innovative work in these fifty years but to expand it.

We have immense tasks ahead of us. They are immense not

only because this country must, as I said, accomplish in fifteen years what has been accomplished in all the previous years of our building of socialism. They are immense also because we must implement our plans through different methods, above all by using the achievements of scientific and technological progress. We have every opportunity to bring about more accelerated advancements. We have well-developed science, a highly skilled working class and farming community and the necessary supplies of raw materials. In short, we have the strength and our people have never lacked a sense of patriotism and creative attitude toward work.

It is important to bring all that into play competently. It has been correctly said here that one must not reduce the incentives for high performance to personal gain. For a working person and, even more so, for progressive workers and innovators, of no lesser and sometimes even of greater importance are moral incentives and recognition of services to society.

At this meeting we have again seen proof of the fact that everything in our work should be done so as to actively enlist all the people, workers of the first rank, first and foremost. The latter, figuratively speaking, are the flower of society. They are people with a great charge of energy, patriotism and responsibility. Who if not they should be involved in working out and adopting national laws and in economic and political decision making? They must be represented in our state bodies throughout, from the highest to the lowest. Their voice must be heard, because it represents the experience of the people. And for this there is no substitute.

In general, we understand our task as follows: To reveal through the new forms of organizational, political and economic work the enormous potential inherent in Soviet people and characteristic of them.

We are striving to develop publicity for our activities in every area of societal life. People should know more about the good and the bad in order to augment the former and implacably combat the latter. This is exactly how it must be under socialism. The cases of glossing over mistakes must be eradicated from our socialist family with a strong hand. In a word, we need healthy work, healthy life, healthy communication, healthy psychology—everything that by its nature is intrinsic to the socialist way of life.

As to the foreign policy of the Party and the Soviet state, we are doing everything to secure peace. You must rest assured that we are approaching this goal with a full awareness of our responsibility.

Comrades! Our meeting has turned out to be a good forum. It is good because you have said many useful and valuable things here. The Party Central Committee will attentively examine your proposals and consider them in its practical work.

Once again our congratulations to you on this anniversary. Thanks again for the enormous work you have done and for your dedication to our cause. I wish you all good health, so that the veterans may work alongside the youth for the glory of our country for many years yet to come. I wish all the best to the young people as well, on whose shoulders today rests the main responsibility for the implementation of our plans. I ask you to convey the wishes of good health and prosperity to your families and fellow workers from the CPSU Central Committee, the Presidium of the USSR Supreme Soviet and the Soviet Government.

September 20, 1985

26

A REPORT
AT THE PLENARY MEETING
OF THE CPSU CENTRAL
COMMITTEE

Report on the Drafts of a New Edition of the CPSU Program, of the Changes in the CPSU Rules, and of the Guidelines for the Economic and Social Development of the USSR for 1986- 1990 and for the Period Ending in the Year 2000. The Report was made at the Plenary Meeting of the Central Committee of the Communist Part of the Soviet Union.

COMRADES,

We shall examine the drafts of an updated edition of the CPSU Program, of the Guidelines for the Economic and Social Development of the USSR for 1986–1990 and for the Period Ending in the Year 2000, and of the changes in the CPSU Rules.

These are documents of immense political significance. They deal with our programmatic objectives, with key questions of the general line of the Party, its economic strategy, forms and methods of work among the masses in the present and an exceptionally complex and important period of history which in many ways, both on the domestic and on the international plane, is one of fundamental change.

As you know, the April Plenary Meeting of the CPSU Central Committee and then the Conference on Problems of Scientific and Technological Progress made a thorough analysis of the existing situation, set forth and substantiated a broad concept for accelerating the country's social and economic development and achieving on this basis a qualitatively new state in Soviet society. This is the crux of the matter and herein lies the whole essence of our problems.

Today our Party sets forth before the people the concept of acceleration of development and with this concept it is proceeding to the next, Twenty-seventh, Congress. This is the core of all the three documents that have been submitted for consideration by the present Plenary Meeting of the CPSU Central Committee. The acceleration of the country's social and economic development is aimed at ensuring a materially and culturally rich and socially dynamic life for the Soviet people in conditions of peace and at bringing out even more fully and vividly the potentialities and advantages of a civilization of an historically new type embodied by the socialist system.

First of all, about the updated edition of the CPSU Program, which has been drafted as instructed by the Twenty-sixth Congress. In the course of serious and thorough work on it there arose far from simple questions of both a theoretical and a political nature, connected with analyzing the results of the road traversed and defining the prospects for the country's further development.

In the past quarter of a century, as we see it, far-reaching economic and social changes of an objective nature have taken place in our country. Such changes required profound analysis, specification of current and long-term goals, definition of ways of attaining them and new approaches to the Party's organizing, socioeconomic and ideological activity. The international situation, too, called for a more precise definition of directives in the Program. We had to work out a new conception of those changes in the alignment of forces that are taking place both on the class and social plane and around the struggle for the affirmation of the principle of peace as a universal norm of interstate and all international relations.

In other words, what was needed was not only to sum up the results of what had been done and accomplished but to draw up a clear and well-substantiated program of action for the sake of humanity and peace on Earth.

What would I like to draw your attention to in this connection?

First of all, to the continuity in the CPSU's basic theoretical and political directives. We attach fundamental importance to this. Life itself has confirmed the correctness of the main content of the Party's Third Program. By fulfilling it, our country has moved far in all areas of communist development. The basic theoretical and political provisions of the Third Program are retained in its updated edition.

The question of continuity in the development of theory and of the Party's programmatic directives is a question of its theoretical adherence to principle and consistency and of its loyalty to Marxism-Leninism. The CPSU would not enjoy such high prestige in the world communist movement and such trust from the Soviet people if it treated its own theoretical conclusions and political appraisals without a proper sense of responsibility.

At the same time, consistency and continuity in theory

definitely presuppose the creative development of that theory, its enrichment with provisions of fundamental importance in accordance with historical experience. This is quite natural. Today we have a better, more precise idea of the ways of perfecting socialism, of achieving the goal stated in our Program—Communism. It goes without saying that all this should have been and was reflected in the Party's main theoretical and political document.

In enriching and developing the content of the Program, we have at the same time critically reassessed those of its formulations which have not stood the test of time. This accords with our Party's traditions. As Lenin pointed out, "criticism of individual points and formulations is quite legitimate and necessary in any live party." [V. I. Lenin, *Collected Works*, vol. 10, p. 31.]

In the whole of this work we proceeded from the Leninist principles of drawing up the Party Program. It should be an exact formulation of the actual process. It should explicitly spell out basic views and political tasks, be free of both excessive detail and groundless fantasy, bookish subtleties and of play with definitions. The Program is an explicit and precise statement of what the Party is seeking to achieve and what it is working for.

The Politburo of the Central Committee believes that the document which has been submitted meets these demands on the whole. It is based on Marxist-Leninist theory, a realistic analysis of the processes taking place in the country and in the world arena, and gives a clear and comprehensive description of the strategic directions of the work of the Party, the Soviet state, and the whole people, proceeding from a communist perspective of the country's development.

The Third Party Program in its present wording is one of planned and all-round improvement of socialism, of a further advancement of Soviet society toward Communism on the basis of accelerating the country's socioeconomic development. It is a program of struggle for peace and social progress.

We are firmly steering a course toward Communism, proceeding from the belief that there is no, nor can there be any sharp divide between the two phases of the single communist formation. It is impossible to go over to the highest stage of Communism directly, bypassing socialism, just as it is wrong to present socialism as an independent social formation. The growth of socialism into Communism is determined by the objective laws of society's development. Any attempts at rushing ahead and introducing communist principles without taking into account the level of the society's material and intellectual maturity are, as experience has shown, doomed to failure. Neither is sluggishness permissible in carrying out necessary transformations and in implementing new tasks.

The updated edition of the Program contains a more comprehensive description of the historic achievements and advantages of socialism as a stage in mankind's progress that excels capitalism and outlines the goals in the economic, social and political spheres and in intellectual life which our society should achieve as a result of implementation of the Program. To attain a qualitatively new state in Soviet society through acceleration of the country's socioeconomic development—such is the formula expressing the substance of the Party's policy today.

The Program proceeds from the decisive role of the economy in society's development. The Party's economic strategy has been determined with due account taken of a further deepening of the scientific and technological revolution. It is aimed at carrying out transformations on a truly historic scale—accomplishing a new technical reconstruction of the economy, transferring it to an intensive path of development and raising the Soviet economy to the highest level of organization and efficiency. And all this is for the sake of the people and for their benefit.

Considerably more attention is given to the social sphere. Our Party must have a socially strong policy, one embracing the whole spectrum of human life—from conditions of work and everyday life, health and leisure to social, class and ethnic relations. In pointing out the need to pay attention to social issues, science and culture, Lenin wrote: "That will be the best policy. That will be the most economical management. Otherwise, while saving a few hundred million, we may lose so much that no sum will be sufficient to restore what we have lost." [V. I. Lenin, *Collected Works*, vol. 29, p. 181.]

It is precisely from this point of view that our attitude to the social sphere is determined in the draft. The Party regards social policy as a powerful means of accelerating the country's economic development and bringing about an upsurge in the labor and sociopolitical activity of the masses as an important factor in ensuring political stability in society, in molding a new human being and in consolidating the socialist way of life.

We attach fundamental importance to the draft's provisions on the development of Soviet society's political system and ever fuller attainment of socialist self-government by the people.

I wish, Comrades, to stress most emphatically that without a comprehensive broadening and deepening of socialist democracy, i.e., without providing conditions for active and effective day-to-day participation of all the working people, their collectives and organizations in resolving matters of state and public life, we will not be able to forge ahead. Lenin regarded as a most important source of strength and vitality of socialism the initiative, energy and creative effort of the people and their conscious and interested attitude to the tasks of building the new system.

The development of genuine power by the people is assuming ever greater significance today, when we are going to carry out most difficult tasks in the field of production, culture and administration. Every real step in ensuring greater openness and publicity, in strengthening control from the grass-roots level, in deepening democratic principles in the activity of all state and public organizations is valuable. In short, we should make maximum use of the democratic nature of socialism and its vital need to draw on the creativity of the masses.

The programmatic tasks in ideological work are also inseparably linked with the acceleration of socioeconomic development. It is necessary to educate people on the ideas of Marxism-Leninism, educate them by word of truth and real deeds, by combining political education and ideological influence with ever-growing participation of working people in the solution of economic and social problems, in the administration of the state, production and public affairs. Only through a well-considered economic strategy, a strong social policy and purposeful ideological and educational work, taken in their inseparable unity, is it possible to activate the human factor, without which none of the tasks put forward can be accomplished. This is how the issue stands today.

The updated edition of the Program also reflects fully enough the main trends in world development. These include a further strengthening of the positions of existing socialism, the growth of its prestige and influence, the increasing role of the popular masses calling for a renewal of life on the principles of justice, growing opposition to positive changes in the world on the part of the reactionary, aggressive forces of imperialism, and a strengthening of the peace potential which unites the countries of socialism, the international working-class and communist movement, scores of newly-free independent states and broad anti-war democratic movements. It is their interaction that determines the general trend in world development in our time.

We can all see that the policy of the major capitalist powers has taken a very dangerous turn. The passage of time, the practical actions of imperialism, especially U.S. imperialism, ever more clearly reveal the essence of this policy, which is one of social revenge on the basis of the achievement of military superiority over socialism, suppression of the progressive and liberation movements, and maintenance of international tensions at such a level as would justify the development of ever new types of mass destruction weapons and the militarization of space.

As a result, international developments have reached a stage which cannot be overcome without taking most important decisions to impose a limit on the arms race and halt the slide toward war. Such decisions cannot be put off lest one should lose control over dangerous processes that threaten mankind's very existence. To curb the forces of militarism and war and ensure a durable peace and reliable security is the cardinal problem of our time.

The search for new approaches to the solution of vitally

important problems, given the tremendous diversity of social and political forces operating in the world arena, demands that a realistic account be taken of often noncoinciding and sometimes even clashing interests so that a correct political course can be worked out. It is the opinion of the Politburo of the Central Committee that the updated edition of the Program provides good pointers in this respect.

It is a complete expression of our concept of strengthening peace on Earth and promoting social progress and national liberation of the peoples. In it are formulated the basic principles of policy, and I would say its principal mainstays, which remain immutable. At the same time, the Program demonstrates our Party's broad approach to international affairs, its ability to take timely account of changes in the situation, to face reality squarely and without prejudice, to assess objectively what is taking place and react flexibly to the demands of the moment.

We openly speak about the objectives of our international policy and about the ways of attaining them. In this sense our policy is quite predictable. There are no riddles or ambiguities in it. It is a policy based on the Leninist idea of the peaceful coexistence of two opposite systems. We proceed from the belief that only a stable and reliable policy is worthy of states and parties that are aware of their responsibility for the future of the world in our age, full as it is of contradictions.

The progressive forces will see in the Program an expression of our invariable solidarity with their struggle, of our respect for their views and stands, of our striving to help consolidate their unity—that dialectic unity of diversity which covers the entire living fabric of the real socialist world, of the working-class, communist and national liberation movements, of all movements against reaction and aggression and for peace and progress.

And now the Draft Guidelines. They are designed to materialize, so to say, the provisions of the CPSU Program, to translate them into the language of concrete plan targets as applied to such a crucial stage in its implementation as the Twelfth five-year plan period and the period till the year 2000.

A great amount of work has been accomplished, but it did not proceed easily or smoothly. And this was not only because the elaboration of a scientifically substantiated perspective for the development of an economy of such an immense scale as ours is not at all a simple thing, and especially now, when it is faced with qualitatively new tasks. We had to take into account the totality of objective factors which in different ways influence the growth rates, proportions and efficiency of the national economy.

We also encountered problems of a different kind, problems stemming from the fact that not all of our cadres have discarded inertia, or given up old patterns and adherence to extensive methods of economic management. Not all, it turned out, are psychologically prepared for work under new conditions, for incorporating in the Twelfth Five-Year Plan a radical turn toward intensiveness and quality. Such moods had to be overcome as we went along while work on the Guidelines was already in full swing. A great role in this respect was played by the fact that work collectives were brought in to help in the search for reserves and in the working out of demanding targets for the five-year plan period and by the fact that Party organizations—from Republican, territorial and regional to local ones—adopted an active position.

As a result, we succeeded in correcting many things, and the draft under discussion today meets in the main, so the Politburo of the Central Committee believes, the demands of the Party Program for speeding up economic growth, and simultaneously carrying out such strategic tasks as improving the people's well-being, strengthening the country's economic potential and maintaining its defense capacity at a proper level.

It is noteworthy that in the new five-year plan the growth in national income and output of all branches of material production will be achieved entirely, for the first time, by raising productivity. A marked reduction in the materials input, envisaged for the five-year plan period, will help turn thrift into a vital source for meeting the requirements of the national economy in additional material resources.

Structural reorganization of the economy and concentration of capital investment on top priority areas of development of the national economy will be effected more energetically than before. Emphasis is laid, first of all, on technical re-equipment and modernization of existing enterprises. The machine building, chemical, electronic and electric engineering industries are to be developed at an accelerated pace. The output of new generations of machinery and equipment and the use of advanced materials and technologies will be expanded.

In short, a marked change toward greater efficiency is envisaged in the Twelfth five-year plan period. But in order to bring about a radical turn in this direction we must not relax our efforts. On the contrary, we must step them up. It is a matter of primary importance to perfect planning and management and methods of running the economy, improve organization, strengthen discipline, enhance responsibility in all sectors and encourage in every way the creative initiative of the masses.

Attainment of the targets to be reached by the start of the Third Millennium will depend on how fast we bring about a turn towards efficiency and carry out a new technical reconstruction of the national economy. It is planned in the next fifteen years to create an economic potential approximately equal in scale to that accumulated throughout all the previous years of Soviet Government and to almost double national income and industrial output. Productivity of labor is to go up by 130-150 per cent.

This will help double the volume of resources for meeting the requirements of the people. I think that the document being presented gives us every ground for saying that the implementation of its social program will make it possible, in the next three five-year plan periods, to raise the Soviet people's standard of living to a qualitatively new level.

The magnitude, depth and complexity of the tasks for both our home and foreign policy make great new demands on the level of Party leadership and dictate the need for new approaches to all aspects of Party work. Naturally, all this must be reflected in the CPSU Rules—the fundamental law of the

Party, its code of life.

What is the basic meaning of the changes proposed for the Party Rules?

Briefly, on the one hand, to further broaden democracy within the Party, develop the initiative and activity of Communists, of all Party organizations, especially primary ones, and, on the other hand, to enhance their sense of responsibility for carrying out common tasks. The more diverse and the richer Party life, the deeper its democratization in decision-making on all key matters—from new admissions to the Party to personnel policy—the stronger and more effective the Party's influence on all social processes.

The basic principles of Party guidance of state and public organizations are defined in the Rules along the same lines. Every one of them is to discharge its functions in full, while Party guidance of their activities should be clearly of a political character and should actively help to further develop socialist self-government of the people in all sectors and at all levels. The proposed changes will help enhance the prestige of the Party member, his importance and role as a political fighter and organizer of the masses and his responsibility for implementing the Party's general line and directives.

On the whole, the proposed changes in the Party Rules will enrich them with new points in accordance with the demands of life, help strengthen the Party organizationally on the basis of the tried and tested principles of democratic centralism and enhance the leading role of the CPSU in the face of new tasks confronting the country.

Comrades, a meeting was held yesterday by the Program Commission which today presents the draft of an updated edition of the Party Program. I believe that our discussion of the draft at the Plenary Meeting will be businesslike and fruitful. What has just been said applies, to no smaller extent, to the Draft Guidelines and the proposed changes in the CPSU Rules.

Adoption by the Central Committee Plenary Meeting of the documents submitted will usher in a very important stage in the preparations for the Twenty-seventh Congress of the

CPSU—a stage of large-scale and direct consultation by the Party with the people on major economic and political matters.

The Politburo proposes that these documents be published and widely discussed at Party meetings, district, city, regional and territorial conferences, and congresses of the Communist Parties of the Union Republics and that the Draft Guidelines should be also discussed at meetings in work collectives, at educational establishments, in army units and public organizations. The Soviets, the trade unions and the Komsomol should also express their views. The participation of millions and millions of Soviet people—Communists and non-Party people—in Party-wide and nation-wide debate will make it better possible to adjust the Party's policy for the future and take fuller account of the will, interests and needs of all classes and of all sections of the people.

It is most important that we should ensure in the process of discussion a businesslike approach and orientation to solving specific practical problems. Meetings and discussions must be meaningful and held without any pomp, fuss and over-organization. The leading Party, state and economic cadres should take a most active and direct part in them.

The work collective and its primary sections—the sector and team, farm and laboratory—should become the center of all work relating to the study and explanation of the pre-Congress documents. Substantive discussions must be held on the questions that concern us, on the need to bring into play our tremendous reserves, on the thrifty use of resources, the removal of existing shortcomings and the spread of advanced experience. It is very important that every person in the Soviet Union should have a clear understanding of the policy objectives and tasks of the Party, of the meaning of its home and foreign policy, and be able to associate his day-to-day work with them.

In other words, it is essential from the very beginning to make the discussion constructive and creative. The Central Committee's line aimed at encouraging an innovative approach to the current problems of our development, at overcoming everything that is outdated and hampers our onward movement, has the total support of the working people. We will continue to pursue this line consistently, relying on the will and creative endeavor of the entire nation.

There is no doubt that the pre-Congress documents will call forth a wave of comments, proposals and letters. Apart from considerations of state importance, people will raise specific issues and make comments on the work of Party, local government and economic bodies. Not a single useful idea, not a single proposal should be left unheeded. It is important that during the discussion of the documents the working people should know that their critical remarks have been heard and appropriate measures are being taken on the basis of their proposals. This is a matter of principle for us.

It seems advisable to use the experience of work on the Guidelines and to draft the five-year plan while the Guidelines are being discussed. This will make it possible to examine and approve it shortly after the Congress.

The concluding stage of the preparations for the Congress makes great demands on the mass media. They should become a nationwide forum for discussion, accumulate the ideas, opinions and experience of the masses and create that lofty labor and ideological-moral atmosphere without which implementation of any plan is impossible.

Comrades, however inspiring the drafted plans may be, the set targets can be achieved only by strenuous and highly efficient work. What is especially needed now are concrete efforts by every Soviet citizen, every work collective, every Party organization. The time has come for still more vigorous actions, and this is the main thing today. It is the duty of Party, local government, economic and trade union organizations to mobilize all our potential, all our resources and possibilities, and, above all the human factor for consistent fulfillment of the set tasks.

We have already started such work. Major decisions have been taken and important measures are being carried out in the economic, social and ideological spheres. We must continue to work in the spirit of the political line we have laid down and undeviatingly follow the course that has been charted. We must continue to speed up our onward movement while improving discipline and order in everything, actively using moral and material incentives and opening still greater prospects for the initiative and creativity of the masses.

All organizing, political and economic efforts, the entire energy of work collectives should be concentrated on completing both the plan for the present year and the five-year plan as a whole with the best results and on approaching in a worthy manner the Twenty-seventh Congress of our Communist Party. This is now the most urgent task, both practically and politically.

Historical experience convincingly shows that the loftiest dream of the happiness of the people, even if it is a dream of a genius, will remain just a noble idea if it does not capture the minds and hearts of millions. On becoming an asset of the popular masses, forward-looking ideas turn into a mighty motive force of progress.

The policy of the Communist Party, its wisdom and conscience, correctly express what is felt and understood by the people—their thoughts, aspirations and hopes. And we are convinced that the great cause of Communism, to which the Party has devoted itself, is invincible.

October 15, 1985

27

A MESSAGE TO
THE SOVIET PEOPLE

A New Year's Message was delivered to the Soviet TV audience on December 31, 1985.

DEAR COMRADES,

Within minutes the Kremlin chimes will ring in the New Year. These are always particularly exciting minutes. It is an old custom for people to pin fresh hopes on the incoming year and sum up the results of the outgoing one. On this day we address our friends, relatives and comrades with New Year's greetings and wish them the very best in life.

It is customary to regard work as the beginning of all beginnings. This is how it really is. I think you'll agree with me when I say that the outgoing year, 1985, will remain in our memories as a year of hard work, bright hopes and bold ambitions for the future.

We all remember very well what difficulties in the national economy confronted us at the opening of this year. We needed the tremendous effort of the entire Party and nation to set matters straight and conclude the year with what has been, in general, not a bad economic performance. The outgoing year serves as a record of everything we have done together for the sake of a better, fairer, and intellectually fuller life and for further strengthening of its socialist foundations and principles.

The outgoing year has been for us a most instructive one, full of events which have speeded up the passage of time, as it were. We have applied ourselves to great undertakings with energy and enthusiasm. Today we have a clearer idea of our potentialities and are more realistic in establishing what we have achieved and what we want to achieve in the future. We want to use the tremendous potential of the socialist system in full measure. This implies qualitative social changes and dynamic and confident movement toward upgrading every aspect of our life, be it economic, cultural, or social.

But, dear Comrades, we are only at the beginning of the road charted by the April Plenary Meeting of the Central Committee of the Communist Party. I would say we are at the very start of a complex endeavor, of major changes that will require us to be yet more persistent and self-sacrificing and fearless in discarding everything that has outlived itself, discarding inert thinking and familiar but useless schemes and approaches. What we need today, above all, is a high degree of social involvement, creative endeavor, intolerance of shortcomings and determined support for everything new, everything advanced that our times bring in.

The essential characteristic of socialism is that it is built by the people and for the people. It relies on the creative potential of the masses. These are the principles which guide the Communist Party in all its activities and initiatives. The Party's Central Committee and the Soviet Government feel active nation-wide support for the economic and political measures recently taken. We highly appreciate this support, being aware of the great responsibility it places upon us and feeling inspired for continued steady movement toward perfecting the society in which we live.

The incoming year of 1986 brings in a new Twelfth Five-Year Plan. We pin on it great hopes for solving many vital problems that arise from the need to accelerate the country's social and economic development.

The forthcoming Twenty-seventh Congress of the Communist Party will be the main political event of the year. The nation-wide discussion of the draft documents which are to be considered at the Congress is under way. At their meetings and in letters to the Central Committee people discuss in a straightforward and businesslike manner the tasks facing the country, the obstacles that hinder our progress and the things that must be done. They declare that the current policy should be continued vigorously and unfailingly. Now we call things by their proper names. We call success *success*, shortcomings *shortcomings* and mistakes *mistakes*. This is an effective medicine for arrogance and self-satisfaction and a key to our further advance, in a creative and friendly atmosphere toward new successes and accomplishments, a new quality of life and new heights of social, economic and cultural development.

In the outgoing year we marked the fortieth anniversary of

the great Victory over Nazism. The memory of the exploit of our people during the years of the war lives on in our minds and in our hearts. And the pain of the losses of that bleak period obliges us to do everything possible to prevent a new global tragedy. The Central Committee of the Communist Party and the Soviet Government, expressing the will of the Soviet people, will do everything they can to preserve peace, avert the threat of a nuclear war and prevent a fatal disaster.

The world today is complex and varied. In its policy the Soviet Union is guided by the awareness of the fact that in the nuclear age the people of the Earth are all in one boat. It is irresponsible to rock this boat with military adventurism. Today life itself rejects political flippancy. For this reason the Soviet Union and the other socialist countries are persistently working for peace and healthier international relations in order to make them civilized, as befits relations between people of the enlightened twentieth century. We must be able to rise above our controversies and focus all efforts on the search for mutual understanding, confidence and disarmament.

The United Nations proclaimed 1986 the International Year of Peace. The Soviet Union wants the Peace Year to grow into the Peace Decade and for humanity to enter the twenty-first century in an atmosphere of peace, confidence and cooperation.

Dear Comrades,

At the dawn of socialism Vladimir Ilyich Lenin said it was happiness ". . . to begin building a Soviet State and thus to begin a new epoch in the history of the world." [V. I. Lenin, *Collected Works,* vol. 33, p. 55.] This was and remains a difficult happiness. We take pride in the fact that our history, life and struggle are inseparable from the history, life and struggle of the human race as a whole for peace and social progress. We pride ourselves on having become pioneers on an untrodden path leading to a new society and on proceeding along it with dignity and confidence.

We send cordial New Year's greetings to our friends and allies, the peoples of the socialist countries! We wish them further success in building a new life.

We congratulate the peoples of friendly states, our class comrades in all the countries of the world.

We wish all nations peace, happiness and prosperity!

On behalf of the Central Committee of the Communist Party of the Soviet Union, the Presidium of the USSR Supreme Soviet and the USSR Council of Ministers, I most warmly and cordially wish all Soviet people, the close-knit family of the peoples of our great homeland, a happy New Year!

New Year's greetings to the working class, the collective farmers, the people's intelligentsia and war and labor veterans!

New Year's greetings to the Soviet officers and soldiers who reliably protect the peaceful work of our people and the gains of the Great October Revolution!

New Year's greetings to all who are at the moment contributing to the labor efforts and defenses of the nation and who are working far from home!

Let us wish each other that the New Year sees our aspirations come true and that it brings fresh success, efficient work, a durable peace and changes for the better. May it be rich in joy and happiness for every home and family!

Happy New Year, dear Comrades!